Annabel Karmel's
New Complete Baby and Toddler Meal Planner

200 quick, easy and healthy recipes for your baby

EBURY PRESS

This book is dedicated to my children, Nicholas, Lara and Scarlett,
and to the memory of my first daughter, Natasha.

10 9 8 7 6 5 4 3 2 1

Text copyright © Annabel Karmel 1991, 1998, 2001, 2004, 2007
Photographs copyright © Ebury Press 2007
This edition copyright © Ebury Press 2007

The right of Annabel Karmel to be identified as the author
of this work has been asserted by her in accordance with the
Copyright, Designs and Patents Act 1988.

This revised edition published for Mothercare in 2007
by Ebury Press, a Random House Group Company
Random House
20 Vauxhall Bridge Road, London SW1V 2SA
www.randomhouse.co.uk

The Random House Group Limited Reg. No. 954009

A CIP catalogue record for this book is available from
the British Library

ISBN: 0-091-90031-X

Design: Smith & Gilmour, London
Illustrations: Nadine Wickenden
Photography: Dave King

Printed in Italy by Graphicom SRL

Contents

Introduction

Weaning your baby is an exciting milestone for any parent. Unfortunately, as soon as you consult family, friends, websites and magazines excitement turns to anxiety. You already feel guilty that you started feeding your baby at 5 months and after 2 weeks of bland, tasteless baby rice you are wondering whether you should venture into the unknown and purée some carrots. But do they contain nitrates? Should they be organic and do you boil or steam them? Should you give carrots for three days, looking for signs of allergy, before moving on to another food? If you freeze portions in ice cube trays should you sterilise the trays first, and is it safe to defrost the cubes in a microwave? And that's just vegetables … When is it safe to give fish, chicken or meat? Feeding a baby soon becomes a world of wonderment and confusion.

How many old wives' tales have you been told? Do you find yourself withholding foods like eggs, meat and fish but not really knowing why? I'm sorry to say that a lot of the advice you are given is not based on any scientific research. My aim is to guide you through feeding your baby, taking each stage month by month, separating truth from fiction, answering all your questions – thereby giving you the confidence to prepare fresh food that will give your baby the very best start in life.

In early childhood, eating habits and tastes (good or bad) are formed for life. Babies grow more rapidly in their first year than at any other time and you have this window of opportunity between six and twelve months where you can develop your baby's taste-buds. This is the time to introduce many different flavours and textures. Move on to meat, chicken and fish after a few weeks – these are vitally important foods in the first year – and start mashing and chopping food early on or your child can get lazy about chewing. If you bring up your child on fresh foods from the start, the transition to family meals will be much easier. Miss this crucial time and your child may join the ranks of picky eaters.

I first wrote this book back in 1991 after the untimely death of my first child Natasha who died due to a rare viral disease. I wanted some good to come from Natasha's short life so I spent many years researching the whole subject of child nutrition, working with top experts in the field. For more than 15 years this has been the leading book on feeding babies and children and has been translated into over 20 languages. This new edition takes in all the latest research in child nutrition, includes new improved versions of the original recipes, 25 brand new recipes and photographs that bring the recipes to life.

With 90 per cent of junk food being bought by parents for their kids and more than one in five under-fours in Britain overweight we need to bring back home cooking. For the past 16 years I've probably spent more time in the kitchen cooking up healthy children's meals than anyone in the country and all the recipes are tested on a panel of babies and toddlers. With a little bit of help from the book, you too can be making really nutritious food that's easy to prepare and plate-lickingly good. I can also promise that you and your kids will love the results without spending hours in the kitchen.

I hope you enjoy the advice and recipes in this book as much as I have enjoyed creating them ...

Annabel Karmel

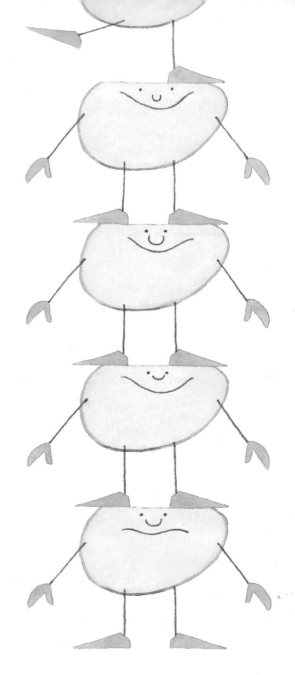

CHAPTER ONE

The best first foods for your baby

The current UK Department of Health recommendations state that babies should not begin weaning until they are six months old and should be exclusively breastfed until this time. However, this has only recently changed from 'between four and six months'. Statistics have shown that the majority of babies in the UK begin weaning before six months, and most health professionals recognise that many babies show signs that they are ready for weaning at a younger age than six months. The very minimum age should be 17 weeks, as a baby's digestive system won't fully mature for the first few months and foreign proteins very early on may increase the likelihood of food allergies.

Milk is still the major food

It is very important to remember, when starting your baby on solids, that milk is still the best and most natural food for growing babies. I would encourage mothers to give breastfeeding a try. Apart from the emotional benefits, breast milk contains antibodies that will help protect infants from infection. In the first few months, they are particularly vulnerable and the colostrum a mother produces in the first few days of breastfeeding is a very important source of antibodies which help to build up a baby's immune system. (If only for this reason, it is obvious that there are some enormous benefits in breastfeeding your child, even for as little as one week.) It is also medically proven that breastfed babies are less likely to develop certain diseases in later life.

Milk should contain all the nutrients your baby needs to grow. There are 65 calories in 120 ml/4 fl oz milk, and formula milk is fortified with vitamins and iron. Cow's milk isn't such a 'complete' food for human babies so is best not started until your baby is one year old. Solids are introduced to add bulk to a baby's diet, and to introduce new tastes, textures and aromas; they also help the baby to practise using the muscles in his mouth. But giving a baby too much solid food too early may lead to constipation, and provide fewer nutrients than he needs. It would be very difficult for a baby to get the equivalent amount of nutrients from the small amount of solids he will consume as he gets from his milk.

Don't use softened water or repeatedly boiled water when making up your baby's bottle, because of the danger of concentrating mineral salts. Babies' bottles should not be warmed in a microwave, as the milk may be too hot even though the bottle feels cool to the touch. Warm bottles by standing them in hot water.

Between four and six months babies should have 500–600 ml/18–21 fl oz breast or infant formula each day. 500 ml/18 fl oz is enough when solids are introduced but it isn't between four and six months with no solids. It's important to make sure that, up to the age of eight months, your baby drinks milk at least four times a day (especially as it is highly likely that a bottle may not be finished at each feed). If the number of feeds is reduced too quickly, your baby will not be able to drink as much as is needed. Some mothers make the mistake of giving their baby solid food when he is hungry, when what he really needs is an additional milk feed.

Babies should be given breast or formula milk for the whole of the first year. Ordinary cow's, goat's or sheep's milk is not suitable as your baby's main drink as it doesn't contain enough iron and other nutrients for proper growth. However, whole cow's milk can be used in cooking or with cereal when weaning. Dairy products like yoghurt, fromage frais and cheese can be introduced once first tastes of fruit and vegetables are accepted and are generally very popular with babies. Choose full-fat products as opposed to low-fat as babies need the calories for proper growth.

Fresh is best

Fresh foods just do taste, smell and look better than jars of pre-prepared baby foods. Nor is there any doubt that, prepared correctly, they are better for your baby (and you), for it is inevitable that nutrients, especially vitamins, are lost in the processing of pre-prepared baby foods. Home-made foods taste different from the jars you can buy. I believe your child will be less fussy and find the transition to joining in with family meals easier if he is used to a wide selection of fresh tastes and textures from an early age.

Organic

Organic fruit and vegetables are produced without artificial chemicals, such as pesticides and fertilisers. However, there is at present no scientific evidence that pesticide levels in ordinary foods are harmful to young babies and children, but some mothers prefer not to take the risk. It is an environmentally friendly option but generates higher prices and it is up to you to decide whether it's worth the extra money.

GM foods

Genetic modification (GM) is the process of transferring genes from one species to another. For example, a tendency to resist damage from certain insects could be implanted from one plant to another. More research is needed to know whether genetic modification can improve the quality and availability of crops or whether the cost to humans and the environment outweighs any benefit. If you wish to avoid GM foods, consult the labels as by 2005 it will be compulsory to declare GM ingredients.

Nutritional requirements

Proteins

Proteins are needed for the growth and repair of our bodies; any extra can be used to provide energy (or is deposited as fat). Proteins are made up of different amino acids. Some foods (meat, fish, soya beans and dairy produce, including cheeses) contain all the amino acids that are essential to our bodies. Other foods (grains, pulses, nuts and seeds) are valuable sources of protein but don't contain all the essential amino acids.

Carbohydrates

Carbohydrates and fat provide our bodies with their main source of energy. There are two types of carbohydrate: sugar and starch (which in complex form provides fibre). In both types there are two forms: natural and refined. The natural form provides a more healthy alternative.

Fats

Fats provide the most concentrated source of energy, and babies need proportionately more fat in their diet than adults. Energy-dense foods like cheese, meat and eggs are needed to fuel their rapid growth and development, and fat provides more than 50 per cent of the energy in breast milk. Foods that contain fats also contain fat soluble vitamins A, D, E and K, which are important for the healthy development of your baby. The problem is that many people eat too much fat and the wrong type.

There are two types of fat – saturated (solid at room temperature) which mainly come from animal sources and from artificially hardened fats found in cakes, biscuits and hard margarines, and unsaturated (liquid at room temperature), which come from vegetable sources. It is the saturated fats which are the most harmful and which may lead to high cholesterol levels and coronary disease later in life.

It is important to give your baby whole milk (full-fat) for at least the first two years but try to reduce fats in cooking and use butter and margarine in moderation. Try to reduce saturated fats in your child's diet by cutting down on fatty meats like fatty minced meat or sausages and replace them with lean red meat, chicken or oily fish.

Essential fatty acids (EFAs) are important for your baby's brain and visual development. There are two types of EFA – omega 6 from seed oils, e.g. sunflower, safflower and corn, and omega 3 from oily fish, e.g. salmon, trout, sardines and fresh tuna (N.B. not tinned tuna). In general we get enough omega 6 in our diets – it is the omega 3 that is often low. The right balance of both types of EFAs are important, especially in early life.

Sugars

Natural

- Fruits and fruit juices
- Vegetables and vegetable juices

Refined

- Sugars and honey
- Soft drinks
- Sweet jellies
- Jams and other preserves
- Biscuits and cakes

Starches

Natural

- Wholegrain breakfast cereals, flour, bread and pasta
- Brown rice
- Potatoes
- Dried beans and lentils
- Peas, bananas and many other fruits and vegetables

Refined

- Processed breakfast cereals (e.g. sugar-coated flakes)
- White flour, breads and pasta
- White rice
- Sugary biscuits and cakes

The Essential Vitamins and Minerals

VITAMIN A
Essential for growth, healthy skin, tooth enamel and good vision. Also boosts the immune system.
Liver
Oily fish
Carrots
Dark green leafy vegetables
(e.g. broccoli)
Orange and red fruit and vegetables
(e.g. carrots, red peppers, sweet potatoes, tomatoes, apricots, mangoes and squash)

VITAMIN B COMPLEX
Essential for growth, for changing food into energy, for a healthy nervous system and as an aid to digestion. There are a large number of vitamins in the B group. Some are found in many foods, but no foods except for liver and yeast extract contain them all.
Meat
Sardines
Dairy produce and eggs
Wholegrain cereals
Dark green vegetables
Yeast extract (e.g. Marmite)
Nuts
Dried beans
Bananas

VITAMIN C
Needed for growth, healthy tissue and healing of wounds as it helps to fight infection. It also helps in the absorption of iron.
Vegetables such as:
broccoli, sweet peppers, potatoes, spinach, cauliflower
Fruits such as:
citrus fruits, blackcurrants, melon, papaya, strawberries, kiwi fruit

VITAMIN D
Essential for proper bone formation, it works in conjunction with calcium. It's found in few foods, but is made by the skin in the presence of sunlight.
Oily fish
Eggs
Margarine
Dairy produce

VITAMIN E
Important for the composition of the cell structure. Helps the body create and maintain red blood cells.
Vegetable oils
Avocado
Wheatgerm
Nuts and seeds

CALCIUM
Important for strong bones, good teeth and growth.
Dairy products
Canned fish with bones
(e.g. sardines)
Dried fruit
White bread
Green leafy vegetables
Pulses

IRON
Needed for healthy blood and muscles. Iron deficiency is very common and will leave your child feeling tired and run down. Red meat is the best source of iron. It's more difficult to absorb iron from non-meat sources. However, if combined with vitamin C-rich foods, iron absorption can be increased by about 30 per cent.
Red meat, especially liver
Oily fish
Egg yolks
Dried fruits (especially apricots)
Wholegrain and fortified cereals
Lentils and dried beans
Green leafy vegetables

For most babies who eat fresh food in sufficient quantities and drink formula milk until the age of one year, vitamin supplements are probably unnecessary. However, in the UK the Department of Health recommends that if your baby is being breastfed (breastmilk doesn't contain enough Vitamin D) or is drinking less than 500 ml/18 fl oz of infant formula a day, you should give him vitamin supplements from the age of six months to two years. Ask your health visitor for advice.

Children following a vegan diet should have at least 600 ml/21 fl oz of a fortified infant soya milk daily until the age of two, then they won't need supplements. It is mainly Vitamins A and D that are likely to be low in children aged six months to two years who don't have 500 ml/18 fl oz fortified infant or soya formula.

Vitamins are necessary for the correct development of the brain and nervous system. A good balanced diet should supply all the nutrients your child needs and an excess of vitamins is potentially harmful, but children who are picky eaters could benefit by taking a multi-vitamin supplement specially designed for children.

There are two types of vitamins – water-soluble (C and B complex) and fat-soluble (A, D, E and K). Water-soluble vitamins cannot be stored by the body, so foods containing these should be eaten daily. They can also easily be destroyed by overcooking, especially when fruits and vegetables are boiled in water. You should try to preserve these vitamins by eating the foods raw or just lightly cooked (in a steamer, for instance).

High-Risk Foods

More and more children are developing an allergy to sesame seeds, so don't give them to highly atopic babies until they're at least nine months. Berry and citrus fruits can trigger a reaction but rarely cause a true allergy. The most common allergic problems that may be triggered by an adverse reaction to food are: nausea; vomiting; diarrhoea; asthma; eczema; hayfever; rashes and swelling of the eyes, lips and face. This is one reason why it's unwise to rush starting your baby on solid foods.

It really isn't necessary to give a very young baby anything to drink other than milk or plain water if he is just thirsty. Fruit syrups, squashes and sweetened herbal drinks should be discouraged, to prevent dental decay. Don't be fooled if the packet says 'dextrose' – this is just a type of sugar.

If your baby refuses to drink water, then give him unsweetened baby juice or fresh 100 per cent fruit juice. Dilute according to instructions or, for fresh juice, use one part juice to three parts water.

Water

Humans can survive for quite a time without food, but only a few days without water. Babies lose more water through their skin and kidneys than adults and also through vomiting and diarrhoea. Thus it's vital that they don't become dehydrated. Ensure your baby drinks plenty of fluids; cool, boiled water is the best drink to give on hot days – it's a better thirst quencher than any sugary drink. Avoid bottled mineral water as it can contain high concentrations of mineral salts, which are unsuitable for babies.

The Question of Allergies

If your family has a history of food allergy or atopic disease such as hayfever, asthma or eczema, there is an increased risk of developing an allergic disorder, so foods should be introduced with great care. If possible, breastfeed exclusively for the first six months. If not, discuss with your doctor the option of using a 'hypoallergenic' infant formula instead. When weaning, start with low allergen foods like baby rice, root vegetables, apple or pear. New foods should be introduced one at a time and tried for two or three days. In that way, if there is a reaction you will know what has caused it. Avoid high-risk foods until your baby is nine to twelve months old.

There's no need to worry about food allergies unless there is a family history of allergy or atopic disease. The incidence of food allergy in normal babies is very small and, with the tendency to a later introduction of solid food at six months, they've become even less common. Don't remove key foods like milk and wheat from your child's diet before consulting a doctor. Many children grow out of their allergies by the age of two, but some – particularly a sensitivity to eggs, milk, nuts or shellfish – can last for life. If your child has an allergy, tell any adults who may feed him.

Never be afraid to take your baby to the doctor if you are worried that something is wrong. Young babies' immune systems aren't fully matured and babies can become ill very quickly if they aren't treated properly and can develop serious complications.

Lactose Intolerance

Lactose intolerance isn't actually an allergy but the inability to digest lactose – the sugar in milk – because of a lack of a digestive enzyme. This can be hereditary and, if this is the case, your child may experience nausea, cramps, bloating, diarrhoea and gas, usually about 30 minutes after consuming dairy foods, and should be given a special diet that avoids all dairy products. Since lactose is present in breast and cow's milk, babies who are lactose intolerant should be given soya formula. However, soya milk isn't recommended for babies under the age of six months, and so these babies should be given a special low-lactose infant formula (sometimes labelled 'LF').

Lactose intolerance is a rare complication that can occur after a gastrointestinal infection. In children over one year, it's safe to remove milk products for a few days to see if this makes a difference. In babies under a year, continue to breastfeed but, if additional feeds are needed, talk to a doctor, health visitor or pharmacist about using a low-lactose feed for a couple of weeks.

If children suffer from lactose intolerance due to a lack of lactase, this will last for life.

Cow's Milk Protein Allergy

If you think your baby is sensitive to cow's milk, you should consult your doctor. Breast milk is the best alternative, but mothers should limit their own consumption of dairy products as they can be transferred to their baby through breast milk. If breastfeeding has ceased, your doctor will recommend an extensively hydrolysed (low-allergen) infant formula, which is available on prescription.

This condition means that no dairy products are tolerated. Milk-free vegetable or soya margarine may be substituted for butter. There are also many soya-based (non-dairy) yoghurts and desserts available and carob can be substituted for milk chocolate. Babies often outgrow this allergy by the age of two, but until then it's important to ensure your child gets enough calcium in his diet.

Eggs

Eggs can be given from six months but they must be thoroughly cooked until both the white and the yolk are solid. Soft-boiled eggs can be given after one year.

Fruits

Some children have an adverse reaction to citrus, berries and kiwi fruit. Rosehip and blackcurrant, being rich in Vitamin C, make good alternatives to orange juice.

Honey

Honey should not be given to children under twelve months as it can cause infant botulism. Although this is very rare, it is best to be safe as a baby's digestive system is too immature to deal with the bug.

Nuts

It is rare to be allergic to tree nuts such as walnuts and hazelnuts. However, peanuts and peanut products can induce a severe allergic reaction – anaphylactic shock – which can be life threatening, so it's best to be cautious. In families with a history of any allergy including hayfever, eczema and asthma, it's advisable to avoid all products containing peanuts, including peanut oil, until the child is three years old, and then seek medical advice before introducing peanut products into the diet. Peanut butter and finely ground nuts, however, can be introduced from six months, provided there is no family history of allergy.

It is important to only buy packaged food that is labelled 'nut free'; loose bakery products, sweets and chocolates may contain nuts. Children under the age of five shouldn't be given whole nuts because of the risk of choking.

Gluten

Gluten is found in wheat, rye, barley and oats. Foods containing gluten, such as bread or pasta, should not be introduced into any baby's diet before six months.

When buying baby cereals and rusks, choose varieties that are gluten-free. Baby rice is the safest to try at first, and thereafter there are plenty of alternative gluten-free products such as soya, corn, rice, millet rice noodles and buckwheat spaghetti, and potato flours for thickening and baking.

In some cases intolerance to wheat and similar proteins is temporary, and children may grow out of the condition before they are two or three years old. However, although it is rare, some people suffer from a permanent sensitivity to gluten known as coeliac disease. Symptoms include loss of appetite, poor growth, swollen abdomen and pale and particularly smelly stools. Coeliac disease can be diagnosed by a blood test and can be confirmed by looking at the gut wall using endoscopy.

Gastro-oesophageal reflux

Reflux is caused when a weak valve at the top of a baby's stomach allows their feed, along with gastric acid, to come back up, causing symptoms including vomiting and heartburn. All babies are born with this weak valve but some regurgitate excessive amounts because of reflux. Regular vomiting, refusing feeds or only managing small amounts at a time, losing or not gaining weight, or crying excessively after feeds can all be symptoms of reflux. If you are worried take your baby to your GP.

If your baby is diagnosed with reflux:

⊛ Holding your baby in an upright position during and about 20 minutes after each feed can help.

⊛ Raising the head end of your baby's cot a few inches off the ground by placing blocks or thick books under the legs of the cot means gravity will help to keep his feed down.

⊛ Try giving smaller, more frequent feeds so as not to overload your baby's stomach.

⊛ In more severe cases it can be worth trying feed thickeners that can be used when breast- or bottle-feeding. There are also several prethickened formulas available on prescription. Some babies also require antacid medicines. Most cases of gastro-oesophageal reflux improve after starting solids but for most babies this is not an indication to start solids early.

Preparing Baby Foods

Preparing and cooking baby foods isn't difficult but, because you're dealing with a baby, considerations like hygiene must be of the utmost importance. Always wash fruit and vegetables carefully before cooking.

Equipment

Most of the equipment you require will already be in your kitchen – mashers, graters, sieves, etc. – but the following four pieces may not be, and I consider them to be vital!

Mouli/baby food grinder (see page 208) This hand-turned food mill purées the food, separating it from the seeds and tough fibres which can be difficult for the baby to digest. It is ideal for foods like dried apricots, sweetcorn or green beans, and is also good for potato, which becomes sticky in a food processor or blender.

Electric hand blender This is easy to clean and ideal for making small quantities of baby purée.

Food processor This is good for puréeing larger quantities when making batches of purées for freezing.

Steamer Steaming food is one of the best ways to preserve nutrients. It is worth buying a multi-tiered steamer, so you can cook several foods at once. (A colander over a saucepan with a well-fitting lid is a cheaper alternative.)

Sterilising

At first, it is very important to sterilise bottles properly, and particularly the teats that your baby sucks, by whatever approved method you choose. Warm milk is the perfect breeding ground for bacteria and, if bottles are not properly washed and sterilised, your baby can become very ill. However, it is not necessary to sterilise the equipment you use for cooking, puréeing or storing baby food, but take extra care to keep everything very clean.

Use a dishwasher if you have one, which helps to ensure the equipment is perfectly clean. Dry utensils with a clean tea towel or use kitchen paper.

All milk bottles and teats should continue to be sterilised until your baby is one year old, but there is really not much point sterilising spoons or food containers beyond the age when your baby starts to crawl and put everything in reach into his mouth. There is no need to sterilise any other feeding equipment, but do wash bowls and spoons in a dishwasher or by hand at about 27°C/80°F – you will need to wear rubber gloves. If using a food mixer it is a good idea to rinse it out with boiling water as they are a common breeding ground for bugs.

Steaming

Steam the vegetables or fruits until tender. This is the best way to preserve the fresh taste and vitamins. Vitamins B and C are water-soluble and can easily be destroyed by overcooking, especially when foods are boiled in water. Broccoli loses over 60 per cent of its antioxidants when boiled, but less than 7 per cent when steamed.

Boiling

Peel, seed or stone the vegetables or fruits as necessary and cut into pieces. Try to use the minimum amount of water and be careful not to overcook. To make a smooth purée, add just enough of the cooking liquid or a small amount of formula or breast milk.

Microwaving

Place the vegetables or fruit in a suitable dish. Add a little water, cover leaving an air vent and cook on full power until tender (stir halfway through). Purée to the desired consistency. Check that it isn't too hot to serve to your baby and stir well to avoid hot spots.

Baking

If you are cooking a meal for the family in the oven, you could use the opportunity to bake a potato, sweet potato or butternut squash for your baby. Prick the chosen vegetable with a fork and bake until tender. Cut in half (remove the seeds from the squash), scoop out the flesh and mash together with some water or milk.

Freezing Baby Foods

As a baby only eats tiny amounts, especially in the early stages of weaning, it saves time to make up larger quantities of purée and freeze extra portions in ice cube trays or small plastic freezer pots for future meals. Thus, in a couple of hours you can prepare enough food for your baby for a month using the weekly menu planners.

Cook and purée the food, cover and cool as quickly as possible. To preserve the quality of the food, it is important that any foods that are to be frozen are covered. You can buy ice cube trays that are made of a flexible material and come with lids (see page 208). It is also best if the container is filled almost to the top rather than leaving a large pocket of air above the food. Food should be stored in a freezer that will freeze food to -18°C/-0.4°F or below in 24 hours.

Once your baby starts eating larger portions, it is a good idea to buy some plastic containers with snap-on lids that are designed for freezing baby food. Always label frozen food with the contents and expiry date.

Thaw foods either by taking them out of the freezer several hours before a meal, heating in a saucepan or defrosting in a microwave. Always reheat foods until piping hot, allow to cool and test the temperature of the food before giving it to your baby. If reheating in a microwave, make sure that you stir the food to get rid of any hot spots.

* Never refreeze meals that have already been frozen; however, if using frozen vegetables or fruit to make baby purées they can be cooked and refrozen.
* Do not heat to defrost and then leave in the fridge to reheat and serve.
* If you have defrosted baby food in the fridge overnight, it should be used within 24 hours. Once reheated use within 1 hour as baby food is a prime breeding ground for bacteria.
* Do not refreeze meals that have previously been frozen. The exception to this is that raw frozen food can be returned to the freezer once it is cooked. For example, cooked frozen peas can be refrozen.
* Sometimes you may need to add liquid when reheating frozen food as it can cause food to dry out.
* Baby foods can be stored in a freezer for up to eight weeks.

Introducing particular foods

I have listed opposite particular foods that you should avoid feeding your baby until a certain age has been reached. This is not an exhaustive list and you should refer to each chapter for more information.

Meal Planners

In the next chapter I've devised some meal planners to help you through the first weeks when you start to wean your baby. The First Tastes Meal Planner shows how to gradually wean your baby onto solids using mainly single ingredient, easily digested fruit and vegetable purées that are unlikely to provoke an allergic reaction. Once your baby has been introduced to these tastes, progress to the After

First Tastes Accepted Meal Planner, which includes combinations of fruit and vegetable purées like carrot and pea or peaches, apples and pears. Adapt the recipes according to what is in season.

These planners are intended only as a guide and will depend on many factors including weight. If your baby's last meal is close to bedtime, avoid giving him anything that is heavy or difficult to digest. This is certainly not the time to experiment with new foods if you both want a good night's sleep.

I have tried to give a wide choice of recipes, although I expect that, in practice, meals that your baby enjoys would be repeated several times – and this is where your freezer will come in handy.

In subsequent chapters, there are meal planners for your baby which you may follow or simply use as a guide. Adapt the charts according to what is in season and what you are preparing for your family. From nine months onwards, you should be able to cook for your baby and family together, perhaps eating the recipes you give your baby for lunch and tea for your own supper, provided you do not add salt to your baby's portion.

In these later charts, I have set out four meals a day, but many babies are satisfied with just three meals as well as some healthy snacks.

Many of the vegetable purées in the early chapters can be transformed into a vegetable soup; and a number of the vegetable dishes can serve as good side dishes for the family. Again, if you give the baby some of the vegetables you are preparing for

the family, make sure they have not been salted. In the later chapters many recipes are suitable for the whole family.

With each recipe are symbols of two faces – one smiling ☺, the other gloomy ☹. If you tick these you will find these useful for recording your successes (or otherwise)! Some recipes also show a snowflake, which means the meal is suitable for freezing.

When can they have . . . ?

Gluten (wheat, rye, barley and oats)
6 months
Citrus fruits
6 months
Well-cooked eggs
6–9 months
Soft eggs, e.g. well-cooked scrambled eggs
from 1 year
Added salt
limited amount from 12 months
Sugar
limited amount from 12 months
Whole cow's milk as a main drink
12 months
Honey
12 months
Paté
12 months
Soft/blue cheese, e.g. Brie/Gorgonzola
12 months
Whole/chopped nuts
5 years

CHAPTER TWO
First-stage weaning

As discussed in chapter one, the current UK Department of Health guidelines state that babies should be exclusively breastfed up to the age of six months. However, most babies in the UK begin weaning between four and six months. Every baby is different, and signs that your baby could be ready to start solids are:

1 She is no longer satisfied by a full milk feed.
2 She is demanding increasingly frequent milk feeds.
3 She may start to wake in the night to feed after a period of sleeping through the night.
4 She is interested in watching others eat.
5 She is able to support her head and neck well when in a sitting position.

N.B. A baby's digestive system is not capable of absorbing foods more complex than baby milk before the age of at least 17 weeks.

Start by offering her very smooth, runny purées of apple, pear, carrot, sweet potato, potato or butternut squash. You can also mix fruits and vegetables with baby rice. Don't expect your baby to eat much at all in the first week. Just offer solids once a day at first and choose a time when you are both relaxed and not in a hurry. She will need to be a little bit hungry but not ravenously so. You may need to give her a little milk to take the edge off her hunger first. Don't rush, try and go at your baby's pace.

A mother's instinct is very powerful, so if you feel she is ready, you are probably right. If she doesn't seem at all interested after a couple of attempts, you could always leave it another few days and then try again. Also bear in mind that one of the reasons for the six-month recommendation is that in underdeveloped countries breast milk is sterile, whereas the introduction of solids early on can lead to infection.

First fruits and vegetables

Very first foods should be easy to digest and unlikely to provoke an allergic reaction.

I find that root vegetables like carrot, sweet potato, parsnip and swede tend to be the most popular with very young babies due to their naturally sweet flavour and smooth texture once puréed. The best first fruits for young babies are apple, pear, banana and papaya, but it's important that you choose fruit that is ripe and has a good flavour, so it's a good idea to taste it yourself before giving it to your baby.

Until recently, the advice given was to introduce each food separately, waiting for three days before introducing another new food. However, unless there is a history of allergy or you are concerned about your baby's reactions to a certain food, there is no reason why new foods should not be introduced on consecutive days, provided you keep to the list in the table.

Take care when introducing solids not to reduce your baby's milk intake, as milk is still the most important factor in growth and development.

It is important to wean your baby on as wide a range of foods as possible. After first tastes are accepted you can introduce all fruit and vegetables (see page 31). However, take care with citrus, pineapple, berry fruits and kiwi fruit as these may upset some susceptible babies.

Best first fruits	Best first vegetables
Apple	Carrot
Pear	Potato
Banana*	Swede
Papaya*	Parsnip
	Pumpkin
	Butternut squash
	Sweet potato

Banana and papaya do not require cooking provided they are ripe. They can be puréed or mashed on their own or together with a little breast or formula milk. Bananas are not suitable for freezing.

Fruit

At first a baby should have cooked purées of fruits like apples and pears, or uncooked mashed banana or papaya. After the first few weeks your baby can graduate to other raw mashed or puréed fruits like melon, peach and plum – these are delicious as long as they are ripe.

Dried fruits can be introduced but in small quantities; although they are nutritious they tend to be laxatives. If you are worried about the use of pesticides, organic fruit and vegetables are available.

Vegetables

Some people prefer to start their babies on vegetables rather than fruit in order to establish a liking for more savoury tastes.

When introducing a baby to solids, it is best to start with root vegetables, particularly carrots, since they are naturally sweet. Different vegetables provide different vitamins and minerals (see chart on page 11) so a variety is of value at later stages.

Many vegetables have quite strong flavours – broccoli, for example – so when solids are fairly well established, you could mix in some potato or baby rice and milk to make it more palatable. Very young babies like their food quite bland.

Note that all fruit and vegetables can also be cooked in a microwave (see page 17 for method).

Rice

Another good first food is baby rice. Mixed with water or breast or formula milk, it is easily digested and its milky taste makes for a smooth transition to solids. Choose one that is sugar-free and enriched with vitamins and iron. Personally I prefer to combine baby rice with fruit and vegetable purées.

Textures

At the very beginning of weaning, the rice and fruit or vegetable purées should be fairly wet and soft. This means that most vegetables, for instance, should be cooked until very soft so that they purée easily. You will probably need to thin out the consistency of the purées, since babies are more likely to accept food in a semi-liquid form. You can use formula or breast milk, fruit juice or boiled water.

As your baby becomes more accustomed to the feel of 'solid food' in her mouth, you can gradually start to reduce the amount of liquid that you are adding to the purées, which will encourage her to chew a little. This should be a natural process as she should want to chew her food as she starts teething (usually between six and twelve months). You could also thicken the purées if necessary with baby rice or some crumbled rusk. As the baby becomes older and solid feeding is established (at the age of about six months), some fruit can be served raw and vegetables can be cooked more lightly (retaining more Vitamin C).

Peel, core and deseed fruits as necessary before cooking and/or puréeing. Vegetables with fibres or seeds should be sieved or put through a mouli for a smooth texture. The husks of leguminous vegetables cannot be digested at this stage.

Quantities

At the very beginning, don't expect your baby to take more than 1–2 teaspoons of her baby rice or a fruit or vegetable purée. For this you should need one portion – in this section, this means one or two cubes from an ice-cube tray.

As your baby gets used to eating solids you may need to defrost three or more frozen food-cubes for her meal, or start freezing food in larger pots.

Drinks

Water is the best drink to offer. But freshly squeezed orange juice is high in Vitamin C, which helps your child to absorb iron. If your baby reacts to orange juice you can offer blackcurrant or rosehip instead. Dilute one part juice to at least five parts cooled boiled water. Diluted juice tastes weak to us but babies don't miss the sweet taste as they haven't been used to it. Try to avoid giving sweet drinks as this will give them a sweet tooth and result in them no longer accepting water.

If you buy commercial fruit juices, they should be unsweetened. But even those labelled 'unsweetened' or 'no added sugar' still contain sugars and acids that can lead to tooth decay. It is important not to let your baby continually sip any fluid except water.

A juicer is a useful machine to have in the kitchen when there is a baby in the house. Many fruits and vegetables can be turned into nutritious drinks.

Tips for introducing solids
1 Make the rice or purée fairly wet and soft at first, using breast or formula milk, an unsweetened juice or cooking water. A handy tip is to mix the purée in the plastic removable top of a feeding bottle (which has been sterilised).
2 Hold your baby comfortably on your lap or sit her in her baby chair. It would be better if both of you were protected against spills!
3 Choose a time when your baby is not frantically hungry and maybe give her some milk first to partially satisfy her – she will then be more receptive to the new idea.
4 Babies are unable to lick food off a spoon with their tongues, so choose a small, shallow plastic teaspoon off which she can take some food with her lips. (Special weaning spoons can be bought.)
5 Start by giving just one solid feed during the day, about 1–2 teaspoons to begin with. I prefer to give this feed at lunch-time.

Fruit and vegetables
FIRST TASTES

Apple

MAKES 5 PORTIONS

Choose a sweet variety of eating apple. Peel, halve, core and chop 2 medium apples. Put into a heavy saucepan with 4–5 tablespoons water. Cover and cook over a low heat until tender (7–8 minutes). Or steam for the same length of time. Purée. If steaming, add some of the boiled water from the bottom of the steamer to thin out the purée.

Apple and Cinnamon

Simmer 2 apples in apple juice or water with a cinnamon stick. Cook as above; remove stick before puréeing.

Pear

MAKES 5 PORTIONS

Peel, halve and core 2 pears, then cut into small pieces. Cover with a little water, cook over a low heat until soft (about 4 minutes). Or steam for the same length of time. Purée. If the pears are very ripe you may not need any water, and after the first few weeks of weaning, you can safely purée ripe pears without cooking. Apple and pear together make a good combination.

Banana

MAKES 1 PORTION

Mashed banana makes ideal baby food. It is easy to digest and rarely causes allergic reactions. Choose a ripe banana and mash very well with a fork to make it as smooth as possible. Add a little boiled water or baby milk if it is too thick and sticky for your baby to swallow.

If your baby is suffering from diarrhoea or a stomach upset, a diet of mashed banana, cooked apple purée and baby rice for a few days is a good remedy.

Papaya

MAKES 4 PORTIONS

Papaya is an excellent fruit to give a very young baby. It has a pleasing sweet taste which is not too strong and blends within seconds to a perfect texture.

Cut a medium fruit in half, remove all the black seeds and scoop out the flesh. Purée, adding a little formula or breast milk if you like.

Cream of Fruit

MAKES 3 EXTRA PORTIONS

Combining a fruit purée with baby milk and baby rice or crumbled rusk can make it more palatable for your baby. In the next few months, when your baby may start eating some other exotic fruits like mango and kiwi fruit, this method of 'diluting' the fruit purées with milk will also make them less acidic.

Peel, core, steam or boil and purée the fruit as described and, for each 4-portion quantity of prepared fruit, stir in 1 tablespoon of unflavoured baby rice or half a low-sugar rusk and 2 tablespoons of baby milk.

Three-Fruit Purée

MAKES 4 PORTIONS

This is a delicious combination of three of the first fruits that your baby can eat.

Mix 1 dessertspoon each of pear and apple purées (see page 26) with half a banana, mashed. You could also use half a raw ripe pear, peeled, cored and cut into chunks. Purée this and the half banana in a blender until smooth, then mix together with the dessertspoon of cooked apple purée.

Carrot or Parsnip

MAKES 4 PORTIONS

Peel, trim and slice 2 medium carrots or parsnips. Place in a saucepan of lightly boiling water, cover and simmer for 25 minutes or until very tender. Alternatively, you can steam them. Drain, reserving the cooking liquid, and purée to a smooth consistency, adding as much of the reserved liquid as necessary.

The cooking time is longer for small babies. Once your baby can chew, cut the cooking time down to preserve Vitamin C and keep the vegetables crisper.

Sweet Potato, Swede or Parsnip

MAKES 4 PORTIONS

Use a large sweet potato, a small swede or two large parsnips. Scrub, peel and chop into small cubes. Cover with boiling water and simmer, covered, until tender (15–20 minutes). Alternatively, steam the vegetables. Drain, reserving the cooking liquid. Purée in a blender adding some liquid if necessary.

Potato

MAKES 10 PORTIONS

Wash, peel and chop 400 g/14 oz potatoes, just cover with boiling water and cook over a medium heat for about 15 minutes. Blend with some cooking liquid or baby milk to make the desired consistency. Alternatively, steam the potatoes and blend with some water from the steamer or your baby's usual milk.

Avoid using a food processor to purée potato as it breaks down the starch and makes a sticky pulp. Use a mouli instead.

You can bake potato or sweet potato in the oven. Preheat to 200°C /400°F/Gas 6 for 1–1¼ hours or until soft. Scoop out the inside and mouli or mash with a little baby milk and a knob of butter.

Cream of Carrot

MAKES 2 PORTIONS

A creamy purée can be made with many different vegetables by adding milk and baby rice. Make a purée with one large carrot (approx. 85 g/3 oz). This should make about 100 ml/3½ fl oz carrot purée (see page 28). Mix 1 tablespoon of unflavoured baby rice with 2 tablespoons of your baby's usual milk. Stir the baby rice mixture into the vegetable purée. Half a low-sugar rusk crushed and mixed with milk will also make a creamy purée. Allow the rusk to soften in the baby milk before mixing it into the vegetable purée of your choice.

Butternut Squash

MAKES 6 PORTIONS

Butternut squash has a naturally sweet flavour that is very popular with babies.

Peel a butternut squash weighing about 350 g/12 oz. Deseed and cut the flesh into 2½ cm/1 inch cubes. Steam or cover with boiling water and simmer for about 15 minutes or until tender. Transfer the squash to a blender and make a purée with a little of the cooking liquid.

Fruit and vegetables
AFTER FIRST TASTES ACCEPTED

Courgette
MAKES 8 PORTIONS

Wash 2 medium courgettes carefully, remove the ends and slice. (The skin is soft so doesn't need to be removed.) Steam until tender (about 10 minutes), then purée in a blender or mash with a fork. (No need to add extra liquid.) Good mixed with sweet potato, carrot or baby rice.

Broccoli and Cauliflower
MAKES 4 PORTIONS

Use 100 g/4 oz of either. Wash well, cut into small florets and add 150 ml/5 fl oz boiling water. Simmer, covered, until tender (about 10 minutes). Drain, reserving the cooking liquid. Purée until smooth, adding a little of the liquid, or baby milk, to make the desired consistency.

Alternatively, steam the florets for 10 minutes for better flavour and retention of nutrients. Add water from the steamer, or baby milk, to make a smooth purée. Broccoli and cauliflower are good mixed with a cheese sauce or root vegetable purée like carrot or sweet potato.

Green Beans

French beans are best since they tend to be the least stringy variety; runner beans should be puréed in a mouli. Wash the beans, top and tail, and remove any stringy bits. Steam until tender (about 12 minutes), then blend. Add a little boiled water or baby milk to make a smooth purée. Green vegetables like beans are good mixed with root vegetables such as sweet potato or carrot.

Potato, Courgette and Broccoli
MAKES 4 PORTIONS

Combining potato with green vegetables makes them more palatable for babies. Peel and chop two medium potatoes (200 g/7 oz). Boil in water below a steamer for about 10 minutes or until soft. Place 25 g/1 oz broccoli florets and 50 g/2 oz sliced courgette in the steamer basket, cover and cook for 5 minutes or until all the vegetables are tender. Drain the potato and purée all the vegetables in a mouli, adding enough baby milk to make a smooth consistency.

Broccoli Trio
MAKES 4 PORTIONS

Peel and chop a medium sweet potato (approx.
200 g/7 oz) and boil for 5 minutes. Place 50 g/2 oz
each of broccoli and cauliflower florets in a steamer
basket above the sweet potato, cover and continue
to cook for 5 minutes. When all the vegetables are
tender, purée them in a blender together with a
knob of butter and enough of the cooking liquid
to make the desired consistency.

Carrot and Cauliflower
MAKES 4 PORTIONS

Combining vegetables makes them more interesting
and, once your baby has got used to carrot and
cauliflower separately, this combination makes
a nice change. Cook 50 g/2 oz carrots, scraped and
sliced, in boiling water for 20 minutes until soft.
After 10 minutes, add 175 g/6 oz cauliflower florets.
Drain the vegetables and purée in a blender. Stir in
2 tablespoons of baby milk.

Mango
MAKES 3 PORTIONS

Peel a ripe mango, removing the stone, and purée
the flesh. No need to cook. Combines well with
mashed banana.

Peach
MAKES 4 PORTIONS

Bring a small saucepan of water to the boil. Cut
a shallow cross on the skin of 2 peaches, submerge
them in the water for 1 minute, then plunge into
cold water. Skin and chop the peaches, discarding
the stones. Either purée the peaches uncooked or
steam first for a few minutes until tender. Peach
and banana are a good combination.

Cantaloupe Melon
MAKES 6 PORTIONS

Cantaloupes are the small, very pale green melons
with orange flesh. They are rich in Vitamins A and
C. Only give ripe melon. Cut in half, remove seeds,
scoop out the flesh and purée in a blender.

Other varieties of sweet melon like Galia or
Honeydew are good too. When your baby is a little
older, properly ripe melon may be eaten in pieces.

Plum
MAKES 4 PORTIONS

Skin 2 large ripe plums as for peaches (see above).
Purée in a blender – the fruit can be puréed
uncooked if soft and juicy or you could steam the
plums for a few minutes until tender. Plums are
good mixed with baby rice, banana or yoghurt.

Dried Apricot, Peach or Prune
MAKES 4 PORTIONS

Many supermarkets stock a selection of ready-to-eat dried fruits. Dried apricots are particularly nutritious, being rich in betacarotene and iron. Avoid buying dried apricots that have been treated with sulphur dioxide or E220 – this preserves their bright orange colour, but this substance can trigger asthma attacks in susceptible babies.

Cover 100 g/4 oz fruit with fresh cold water, bring to the boil and simmer until soft (about 5 minutes). Drain, remove the stones and press through a mouli to remove the rough skins. Add a little of the cooking liquid to make a smooth purée.

This is good combined with baby rice and milk, banana or ripe pear.

Apricot and Pear
MAKES 8 PORTIONS

Roughly chop 50 g/2 oz ready-to-eat dried apricots and put them into a saucepan with 2 ripe Conference pears (350 g/12 oz) peeled, cored and cut into pieces. Cook, covered, over a low heat for 3–4 minutes. Purée in a blender. Alternatively, use 4 fresh, sweet, ripe apricots, peeled, stoned and chopped.

Apple and Raisin Compote
MAKES 8 PORTIONS

Heat 3 tablespoons of fresh orange juice in a saucepan. Add 2 eating apples peeled, cored and sliced, and 15 g/½ oz of washed raisins. Cook gently for about 5 minutes until soft, adding a little water if necessary.

Dried fruit like apricots or raisins should be put through a mouli for young babies, to get rid of the outer skin which is difficult to digest.

Peas
MAKES 4 PORTIONS

I tend to use frozen peas as they are just as nutritious as fresh. Cover 100 g/4 oz peas with water, bring to the boil and simmer, covered, for 4 minutes until tender. Drain, reserving some cooking liquid. Purée using a mouli or press through a sieve and add some of the cooking liquid to make the desired consistency. Good combined with potato, sweet potato, parsnip or carrot. If using fresh peas, cook them for 12–15 minutes.

Sweet Red Pepper

MAKES 2–3 PORTIONS

Wash, core and deseed a medium red pepper.
Cut into quarters and roast under a preheated grill
until the skin is charred. Place in a plastic bag and
allow to cool. Peel off the blistered skin and purée.
Good with cauliflower, sweet potato or potato.

Avocado

MAKES 1 PORTION

Cut a well-ripened avocado in half and scoop out
the stone. Use 1/3–1/2 and mash the flesh with a fork,
maybe adding a little milk. Serve quickly to avoid it
turning brown. Good mixed with mashed banana.

Do not freeze avocados.

Corn on the Cob

MAKES 2 PORTIONS

Remove the outer corn husks and silk from the corn
on the cob and rinse well. Cover with boiling water
and cook over a medium heat for 10 minutes. Strain
and then remove the kernels of corn using a sharp
knife. Purée in a mouli. Alternatively, cook some
frozen corn and then purée.

Spinach

MAKES 2 PORTIONS

Wash 100 g/4 oz spinach leaves very carefully,
removing the coarse stalks. Either steam the spinach
or put in a saucepan and sprinkle with a little water.
Cook until the leaves are wilted (about 3–4 minutes).
Gently press out any excess water. Good combined
with potato, sweet potato or butternut squash.

Tomatoes

MAKES 2–3 PORTIONS

Plunge 2 medium tomatoes in boiling water for
30 seconds. Transfer to cold water, skin, deseed
and roughly chop. Melt a knob of butter in a heavy-
bottomed saucepan and sauté the tomato until
mushy. Purée in a blender. This is good combined
with potato, cauliflower or courgette.

Peach and Banana ☺☹

This is a delicious purée to make when peaches are in season. They are a good source of Vitamin C and are easy to digest. Banana also combines well with papaya.

MAKES 1 PORTION
1 ripe peach, skinned and cut into pieces
1 small banana, peeled and sliced
½ tablespoon pure apple juice
baby rice (optional)

Put the peach, banana and apple juice into a small pan, cover and simmer for 2–3 minutes. Purée in a blender. If it's too runny, add a little baby rice.

Three-fruit Purée ☺☹

This makes a nice change from plain mashed banana or apple purée. When your baby is six months or older, you can make this with raw grated apple and mashed banana.

MAKES 1 PORTION
¼ apple, peeled, cored and chopped
¼ banana, peeled and chopped
1 teaspoon orange juice

Steam the apple until tender (about 7 minutes), then purée or mash it together with the banana and orange juice. Serve as soon as possible.

Peaches, Apples and Pears ❄ ☺ ☹

When peaches aren't in season you can make this just using apples and pears. If the purée is too thin, stir in some baby rice to thicken it.

MAKES 8 PORTIONS
2 eating apples, peeled, cored and chopped
1 vanilla pod
2 tablespoons apple juice or water
2 ripe peaches, skinned and chopped
2 ripe pears, peeled, cored and chopped

Put the chopped apple in a saucepan. Split the vanilla pod with a sharp knife, scrape the seeds into the pan and add the pod and apple juice or water. Simmer, covered, for about 5 minutes. Add the peaches and pears and cook for 3–4 minutes more. Remove the pod and purée.

Mixed Dried-Fruit Compote ❄ ☺ ☹

Dried fruit concentrates the goodness of the original fruit. Dried apricots and prunes are a good source of iron and dried apricots are also rich in betacarotene. Their natural sweetness makes them good first foods and I like to mix them with fresh fruit. Prunes are a well-known laxative, so they are good mixed with apple or pear if your baby is constipated.

MAKES 6 PORTIONS
50 g/2 oz each dried apricots, dried peaches and prunes
1 eating apple and 1 pear, peeled, cored and chopped, or 1 apple
   and 3 fresh apricots, skinned, stoned and chopped

Put the dried fruit, apple and pear (or apricot, if using) into a saucepan and just cover with boiling water. Simmer for about 8 minutes. Drain the fruit and purée, adding a little of the cooking liquid if necessary.

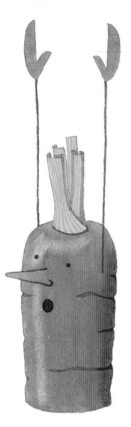

Vegetable Stock ❄ ☺ ☹

Vegetable stock forms the basis of many vegetable recipes. This should keep for a week in the fridge and it is well worth making your own, which will be free from additives and salt.

MAKES ABOUT 900 ML/1½ PINTS
1 large onion, peeled
125 g/4½ oz carrot, peeled
1 celery stalk
175 g/6 oz mixed root vegetables (sweet potato,
*   swede, parsnip), peeled*
½ leek
25 g/1 oz butter
1 sachet bouquet garni
1 sprig of fresh parsley and 1 bay leaf
6 black peppercorns
900 ml/1½ pints water

Chop all the vegetables. Melt the butter in a large saucepan and sauté the onion for 5 minutes. Add the remaining ingredients and cover with the water. Bring to the boil and simmer for about 1 hour. Strain the stock and squeeze any remaining juices from the vegetables through a sieve.

Carrot and Pea Purée ☺ ☹

Both carrots and peas have a naturally sweet taste that appeals to babies.

MAKES 2 PORTIONS
200 g/7 oz carrots, peeled and sliced
40 g/1½ oz frozen peas

Put the sliced carrots in a saucepan and cover with boiling water. Cook, covered, for 15 minutes. Add the peas and cook for a further 5 minutes. Purée with sufficient cooking liquid to make a smooth purée.

Baby Cereal and Vegetables ❄ ☺ ☹

Sometimes vegetable purées can be very watery – here I have added baby rice, which makes an excellent thickening agent.

MAKES 6 PORTIONS
25 g/1 oz onion, peeled and chopped
1 teaspoon olive oil
1 medium courgette, trimmed and sliced
50 g/2 oz broccoli
2 medium carrots, peeled and sliced
vegetable stock (optional)
50 g/2 oz frozen peas
3 tablespoons baby rice

Sauté the onion in the olive oil for 2 minutes, then add all the vegetables except the frozen peas. Just cover with boiling water or vegetable stock. Bring back to the boil, then simmer for 20 minutes. Add the frozen peas and cook for 5 minutes more. Purée the vegetables, adding as much of the cooking liquid as necessary to make the desired consistency, and stir in the baby rice.

Sweet Vegetable Medley ❄ ☺ ☹

Root vegetables like swede, carrot and parsnip make delicious and nutritious purées for young babies. You could also use butternut squash and pumpkin.

MAKES 5 PORTIONS
100 g/4 oz carrot, peeled and chopped
100 g/4 oz swede, peeled and chopped
100 g/4 oz potato, butternut squash or pumpkin, peeled and chopped
50 g/2 oz parsnip, peeled and chopped
300 ml/10 fl oz water or milk (can use cow's milk in cooking from six months)

Put the vegetables in a saucepan with the water or milk. Bring to the boil, then cover and simmer for 25–30 minutes or until the vegetables are tender. Remove with a slotted spoon and purée the vegetables in a blender, together with as much cooking liquid as necessary to make the desired consistency.

Watercress, Potato and Courgette Purée ❄ ☺ ☹

Watercress is rich in calcium and iron. It blends well with the other vegetables to make a tasty, bright green purée. You can add a little milk if your baby prefers it that way.

MAKES 6 PORTIONS
1 large potato (approx. 300 g/11 oz), peeled and chopped
300 ml/10 fl oz vegetable stock (see page 38)
1 medium courgette (approx. 100 g/4 oz), trimmed and sliced
a small bunch of watercress
a little milk (optional)

Put the potato into a saucepan, cover with the stock and cook for 5 minutes. Add the sliced courgette and continue to cook for another 5 minutes. Trim the stalks of the watercress, add to the potato and cook for 2–3 minutes. Purée the mixture in a mouli and, if you like, add a little milk to adjust the consistency.

Avocado and Banana or Papaya ☺ ☹

This is very simple to make and the fruits blend well.

MAKES 1 PORTION
½ small avocado
½ small banana or ¼ papaya

Remove the flesh from the avocado and mash with the banana or papaya until smooth. This should be eaten soon after it is made or the avocado will turn brown.

Butternut Squash and Pear ❄ ☺ ☹

Butternut squash is one of the more unusual vegetables now available in supermarkets. It is easily digested, rarely causes allergies, and is a good source of Vitamin A. Babies like its naturally sweet taste, which combines well with fruit; and cooking fruit and vegetables in a steamer, as here, is one of the best ways of preserving nutrients. Butternut squash is also delicious if you cut it in half, scoop out the seeds, brush each half with melted butter, and spoon 1 tablespoon of fresh orange juice into each cavity. Cover with foil and bake in the oven at 180°C/350°F/Gas 4 for 1½ hours or until tender.

MAKES 4 PORTIONS

1 medium butternut squash or pumpkin (about 450 g/1 lb)
1 ripe juicy pear

Peel the butternut squash, cut in half, remove the seeds and chop into pieces. Steam for about 12 minutes. Peel, core and chop the pear, add to the steamer and continue to cook for 5 minutes or until the squash is tender. Puree in a blender.

Sweet Potato with Cinnamon ❄ ☺ ☹

The addition of cinnamon gives this an extra sweetness, which babies love. This is very simple to make. Sweet potato is also good mixed with a little fresh orange juice.

MAKES 4 PORTIONS

1 sweet potato (about 175 g/6 oz), peeled and cut into chunks
a generous pinch of ground cinnamon
a few tablespoons baby milk

Cover the sweet potato chunks with water, bring to the boil and simmer for about 30 minutes or until soft. Drain and mash together with the cinnamon and enough baby milk to make the desired consistency.

Leek, Sweet Potato and Pea Purée ❄ ☺ ☹

Sweet potatoes make perfect baby food; they are full of nutrients and have a naturally sweet taste and smooth texture. Choose the orange-fleshed variety as it is rich in betacarotene. It is fine to use frozen vegetables in baby purées as they are frozen within hours of being picked and can be just as nutritious as fresh vegetables. Once cooked, frozen vegetables can be refrozen.

MAKES 5 PORTIONS

50 g/2 oz leek, washed and sliced
400 g/14 oz sweet potato, peeled and chopped
300 ml/10 fl oz vegetable stock
50 g/2 oz frozen peas

Put the leek and chopped sweet potato in a saucepan, pour over the vegetable stock and bring to the boil. Cover and simmer for 15 minutes. Add the peas and continue to cook for 5 minutes. Purée in a blender.

First tastes meal planner

Week 1	Early morning	Breakfast	Lunch	Tea	Bedtime
Days 1–2	Breast/bottle	Breast/bottle	Breast/bottle, Baby rice	Breast/bottle	Breast/bottle
Days 3–4	Breast/bottle	Breast/bottle	Breast/bottle Root Vegetable e.g. carrot or sweet potato	Breast/bottle	Breast/bottle
Day 5	Breast/bottle	Breast/bottle	Breast/bottle Pear with baby rice	Breast/bottle	Breast/bottle
Day 6	Breast/bottle	Breast/bottle	Breast/bottle Apple	Breast/bottle	Breast/bottle
Day 7	Breast/bottle	Breast/bottle	Breast/bottle Vegetable e.g. butternut squash or sweet potato	Breast/bottle	Breast/bottle
Week 2					
Days 1–2	Breast/bottle Apple or pear with baby rice	Breast/bottle	Breast/bottle Root Vegetable e.g. potato, parsnip or carrot	Breast/bottle	Breast/bottle
Days 3–4	Breast/bottle Banana or papaya	Breast/bottle	Breast/bottle **Sweet Vegetable Medley**	Breast/bottle	Breast/bottle
Days 5–6	Breast/bottle Apple or pear	Breast/bottle	Breast/bottle Sweet potato, butternut squash or swede	Breast/bottle	Breast/bottle
Day 7	Breast/bottle Peach and banana or mashed banana	Breast/bottle	Breast/bottle Carrot or carrot and parsnip	Breast/bottle	Breast/bottle

Week 3	Early morning	Breakfast	Lunch	Tea	Bedtime
Day 1	Breast/bottle	Breast/bottle Banana	Diluted juice or water **Sweet Vegetable Medley**	Breast/bottle	Breast/bottle
Day 2	Breast/bottle	Breast/bottle Apple	Diluted juice or water **Sweet Vegetable Medley**	Breast/bottle	Breast/bottle
Day 3	Breast/bottle	Breast/bottle **Peaches, Apples and Pears**	Diluted juice or water **Broccoli Trio**	Breast/bottle	Breast/bottle
Day 4	Breast/bottle	Breast/bottle **Cream of Fruit**	Diluted juice or water **Butternut Squash and Pear**	Breast/bottle	Breast/bottle
Day 5	Breast/bottle	Breast/bottle **Cream of Fruit**	Diluted juice or water **Butternut Squash and Pear**	Breast/bottle	Breast/bottle
Day 6	Breast/bottle	Breast/bottle Banana or papaya	Diluted juice or water **Potato, Courgette and Broccoli**	Breast/bottle	Breast/bottle
Day 7	Breast/bottle	Breast/bottle Pear or baby rice	Diluted juice or water **Carrot and Pea Purée**	Breast/bottle	Breast/bottle

These charts are intended only as a guide and will depend on many factors including weight. Some babies may only want one solid feed a day and some may prefer to have a second meal at teatime. Bold type indicates recipes shown in the book.

Fruit juice should be diluted at least three parts water to one part juice, or substituted completely with cooled boiled water.

After first tastes accepted meal planner

	Early morning	Breakfast	Lunch	Tea	Bedtime
Day 1	Breast/bottle	Breast/bottle **Three-Fruit Purée**	**Leek, Sweet Potato and Pea Purée** Breast/bottle	**Carrot and Cauliflower** Water or juice*	Breast/bottle
Day 2	Breast/bottle	Breast/bottle **Three-Fruit Purée**	**Leek, Sweet Potato and Pea Purée** Breast/bottle	**Sweet Vegetable Medley** Water or diluted juice	Breast/bottle
Day 3	Breast/bottle	Breast/bottle Pear and baby cereal	**Broccoli Trio** Breast/bottle	Sweet potato Water or juice*	Breast/bottle
Day 4	Breast/bottle	Breast/bottle **Apple and Cinnamon**	**Baby Cereal and Vegetables** Breast/bottle	Sweet potato Water or diluted juice	Breast/bottle
Day 5	Breast/bottle	Breast/bottle Mango and baby cereal	**Avocado and Banana** Breast/bottle	**Carrot and Pea Purée** Water or juice*	Breast/bottle
Day 6	Breast/bottle	Breast/bottle Banana	**Watercress, Potato and Courgette Purée** Breast/bottle	**Broccoli Trio** Water or diluted juice	Breast/bottle
Day 7	Breast/bottle	Breast/bottle **Apple and Banana with Orange Juice**	**Watercress, Potato and Courgette Purée** Breast/bottle	**Broccoli Trio** Water or juice*	Breast/bottle

These charts are intended only as a guide and will depend on many factors including weight. Some babies will manage to eat some fruit after lunch and tea.

* Fruit juice should be diluted at least three parts water to one part juice, or substituted completely with cooled boiled water.

	Breakfast	Mid-morning	Lunch	Mid-afternoon	Tea	Bedtime
Day 1	Breast/bottle Baby cereal Mashed banana	Breast/bottle	**Leek, Sweet Potato and Pea Purée** Water or juice*	Breast/bottle	Carrot, Mango or Peach, Rusk Water or juice*	Breast/bottle
Day 2	Breast/bottle Baby cereal **Apple and Raisin Compote**	Breast/bottle	Avocado and Banana Water or juice*	Breast/bottle	**Carrot and Pea Purée** Cantaloupe melon Water or juice*	Breast/bottle
Day 3	Breast/bottle Baby cereal Mango and banana	Breast/bottle	**Sweet Potato with Cinnamon** Water or juice*	Breast/bottle	Potato, Courgette and Broccoli Yogurt Water or juice*	Breast/bottle
Day 4	Breast/bottle Baby cereal Fromage frais	Breast/bottle	**Broccoli Trio** Water or juice*	Breast/bottle	**Sweet Vegetable Medley** Mango or papaya Water or juice*	Breast/bottle
Day 5	Breast/bottle Baby cereal **Peaches, Apples and Pears**	Breast/bottle	**Broccoli Trio** Water or juice*	Breast/bottle	**Sweet Vegetable Medley** Fingers of toast Yoghurt Water or juice*	Breast/bottle
Day 6	Breast/bottle Baby cereal **Peaches, Apples and Pears**	Breast/bottle	**Watercress, Potato and Courgette Purée** Water or juice*	Breast/bottle	**Leek, Sweet Potato and Pea Purée** Banana Water or juice*	Breast/bottle
Day 7	Breast/bottle Baby cereal **Apricot and Pear**	Breast/bottle	**Carrot and Pea Purée** Water or juice*	Breast/bottle	Watercress, Potato and Courgette Purée Peach and Banana Water or juice*	Breast/bottle

CHAPTER THREE

Second-stage weaning

Between seven and nine months is a rapid development period for your baby. A seven-month-old baby still needs to be supported whilst you are feeding him and, more often than not, still has no teeth. A nine-month-old baby, however, is usually strong enough to sit in a high chair whilst he is being fed and has already cut a few teeth. Babies of eight months are usually quite good at holding food themselves and enjoy eating small finger foods like pasta, pieces of raw or cooked vegetables or raw fruits. (Turn to pages 95–7 for suitable finger foods for young babies.) Babies are born with a store of iron that lasts for about six months. After this they rely on their diet for the iron they need. If a baby doesn't have at least 500 ml/18 fl oz breast milk or infant formula per day, his daily intake of iron is likely to be below the recommended level, and this can impair his mental and physical development. It is particularly important not to use ordinary cow's milk for your baby's regular drink before the age of one year as it doesn't contain as much iron or vitamins as formula milk.

Less Milk, More Appetite

Once your baby is seven to eight months old, you can start cutting down on his milk so that he is more hungry for his solids. However between six months and one year babies should have 500–600 ml/18–21 fl oz breast milk or infant formula per day. In addition you can give other dairy products and offer water, diluted fruit juice or low-sugar herbal drinks with meals if your baby seems thirsty.

It is best to only put formula, breast milk or water into your baby's bottle. Comfort-sucking on sweetened drinks is the main cause of tooth decay in young children, and babies are more vulnerable to decay than children or adults. You should start using a lidded cup with a soft spout and easy-to-hold handles once your baby is six months old. There are training cups available to guide your baby from a soft spout to open drinking cup in easy stages.

Let your baby's appetite determine how much he eats and never force him to eat something he actually dislikes. Don't offer it for a while, but reintroduce it a few weeks later. You may find that second time around he loves it.

Remember, at this age it is normal for babies to be quite chubby. As soon as your baby starts crawling and walking, he will lose this excess weight.

For those babies who dislike milk and are drinking less than 600 ml (21 fl oz) use milk in recipes like Cauliflower Cheese (page 67). Also a small children's-size pot of yoghurt or a matchbox-size piece of cheese is equivalent to 60 ml (2 fl oz) milk.

Although a low-fat diet is fine for adults, it is not appropriate for young children who need calories to grow. Give whole milk and avoid low-fat dairy products in the first two years.

The Foods to Choose

Your baby can now eat protein foods like eggs, cheese, pulses, chicken and fish. Limit some foods which might be indigestible – such as spinach, lentils, cheese, berry or citrus fruit – and don't worry if some foods, like pulses, peas and raisins, pass through your child undigested: until they are about two years old, babies cannot completely digest husked vegetables and the skins of fruits. Peeling, mashing and puréeing fruit and vegetables will of course aid digestion. With foods like bread, flour, pasta and rice, try to choose wholegrain, rather than refined, as it is more nutritious.

Once your baby has passed the six-month stage and is happily eating bread and other foods containing gluten, there is no longer any need to give him special baby cereals. You can use adult cereals like Ready Brek, instant porridge and Weetabix, which are just as nutritious and much cheaper. Choose a cereal that isn't highly refined and which is low in sugar and salt. Many people continue to use commercial baby foods because they think, due to the long list of vitamins and minerals on the packet, that they are more nutritious. However, babies who eat a good balanced diet of fresh foods get a perfectly adequate quantity of vitamins and minerals. Also, baby foods in general are heavily processed, and their finer texture and bland flavours will hinder the development of your baby's tastes.

Beware, too, of some of the rusks you can buy which are supposedly the 'ideal food for your baby'. Many are full of sugar (some contain more sugar than a doughnut). Give your baby some toast to chew on or follow the simple recipe for rusks in the nine-to-twelve-month finger food section (see page 95).

Ordinary cow's milk isn't suitable as your baby's main drink for the first year, as it doesn't contain enough iron or other nutrients for proper growth. However, whole cow's milk can be used in cooking or with cereal.

It is very difficult to give portion sizes as the quantities that babies eat vary enormously. The amount of food one baby needs to eat to maintain the same growth rate can be very different to the next baby, even if they are the same age and weight. They have different metabolic rates and different activity levels and the food that their parents make can vary in calorie content significantly. The amount a baby eats can also vary from week to week and this is perfectly normal. By seven months babies should ideally be having three solid meals a day. It's a good idea to take your child to be weighed regularly by your health visitor. If she is growing along one centile line on her growth chart and not crossing up or down lines, then she is eating the right amount – this is because babies can drop a couple of lines then grow along a lower one, leading to abnormal growth and failure to fulfil their genetic potential.

Fruit

Your baby should now be able to eat all fruits, and both fresh and dried fruits make a great snack. Different fruits contain different vitamins, so include as much variety as possible. Dried fruits are also a good source of other nutrients and energy. Take care to remove any stones before giving fruit, and don't give whole grapes to young babies as they may choke on them.

Vitamin C boosts iron absorption so it's important to include Vitamin C-rich fruits like citrus or berry fruits in your child's diet. It's good to give cereal with diluted orange juice in the morning. Orange juice also combines well with savoury foods like carrot, fish and liver. To begin with, give berry and citrus fruits in small quantities as they can be indigestible, and some babies can have an adverse reaction to them. Combine them with other fruits like apple, banana, pear or peach. Kiwi fruit can also cause an allergic reaction in some young children. This is rare, but do watch your baby closely, especially if there is a family history of allergies or conditions such as eczema or asthma.

Vegetables

Your baby is now able to eat all vegetables, but if certain flavours – like that of spinach or broccoli – are too strong, try mixing them together with a cheese sauce or with root vegetables like sweet potato, carrot or potato. Combinations of vegetables and fruit are also good – try butternut squash and apple, or spinach and pear. Steamed vegetables, like carrot sticks or small florets of cauliflower, make good finger food.

Frozen vegetables are frozen within hours of being picked, thus sealing in all the nutrients, so it's absolutely fine to use them to make your baby's purées. Whilst you cannot thaw and refreeze frozen foods, e.g. baby purées, this does not apply to frozen vegetables; you can use these to make baby purées and then refreeze them.

Eggs

Eggs are an excellent source of protein and also contain iron and zinc. They can be given from six months, but don't serve raw or lightly cooked eggs

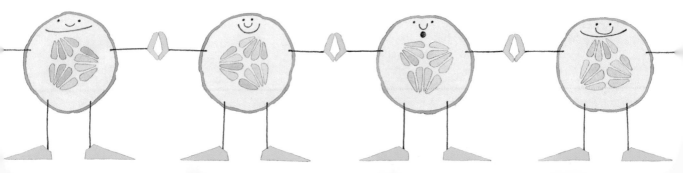

to babies under one year as there is a risk of salmonella. The white and yolk should be cooked until solid. Hard-boiled eggs, omelettes and well-cooked scrambled eggs are quick to cook and nutritious.

A vegetarian diet

A vegetarian diet can be fine for babies and small children as long as it is carefully balanced and does not contain too much fibre. Unlike adults, a bulky high-fibre diet is unsuitable for children as it is too low in calories and essential fats and hinders their absorption of iron. The nutrients that you will need to pay extra attention to are protein, iron, zinc and the B vitamins – these are usually provided by meat. Below is a list of foods that you should include in a vegetarian baby's diet:

Dairy products, eggs, beans, lentils, fortified breakfast cereals, beans and pulses e.g. lentils, soya e.g. tofu, green vegetables e.g. spinach and broccoli, dried fruit

Fish

Many children grow up disliking fish as they find it bland and boring, so I try to mix it with stronger tastes, like salmon with carrots, tomato and grated Cheddar or my tasty combination of fillets of cod with grated cheese, orange juice and crushed cornflakes (believe me, it's yummy). If your child gets excited at the prospect of fish for dinner, then you deserve to be a very proud parent indeed.

If fish is overcooked it becomes tough and tasteless. It is cooked when it just flakes with a fork but is still firm. Always check very carefully for bones before serving.

It's hard to find jars of purée containing fish; however, oily fish like salmon, trout, fresh tuna and sardines are particularly important for the development of a baby's brain, nervous system and vision and ideally should be included in the diet twice a week. Fats are a major component of the brain – for this reason, 50 per cent of the calories of breast milk are composed of fat.

Meat

Chicken is an ideal first meat. It blends well with root vegetables like carrot and sweet potato, which give chicken purée a smoother texture. Chicken also works well with fruits like apple and grape. Home-made chicken stock forms the basis of many recipes so I recommend that you make large batches. It will keep in the fridge for 3–4 days. However, do not use frozen stock to make purées and then refreeze it. You can buy unsalted, ready-made stock.

As well as chicken breast try also using the thigh meat – the dark meat of chicken contains twice as much iron and zinc as the white.

Iron deficiency anaemia is the most common nutritional problem during early childhood, the symptoms of which can be hard to detect: your baby may just be tired and pale and more prone to infection, or his growth and development may seem to slow down. Red meat provides the best source of iron, particularly liver, which is ideal for babies as it has a soft texture and is easy to digest. Babies often reject red meats, not because of the taste but the chewy texture. It's a good idea to combine it with root vegetables or pasta, as they help to produce a texture that is much smoother and easier to swallow.

Iron is important for your baby's brain development, especially between six months and two years. The iron a baby inherits from his mother runs out at around six months. A baby's brain triples in size in the first year and a deficiency in iron can have a profound effect on learning later in life. In the UK one in five babies aged ten to twelve months has daily intakes of iron below the desired level.

Pasta

Pasta tends to be a favourite with babies and young children. It's a good source of carbohydrate and adding tiny pasta shapes to purées when your baby is about eight months is a good way to encourage chewing. Many vegetable purées make good pasta sauces, to which you could add a little grated cheese. Buy tiny pasta shapes like stars or shells (see page 208). Also try couscous, which has a soft texture perfect for babies. It is quick to cook and combines well with diced chicken or vegetables.

Textures

Problems with lumps are very common. Babies who are fed exclusively on jars often have a really difficult time progressing from smooth stage 1 foods to stage 2 jars which often contain quite large lumps like whole peas.

This is too sudden a transition for them. It is important to introduce texture and small lumps as early as possible as the older they are, the harder babies will find it to accept lumpy food. This makes the transition to eating normal family meals a very difficult one and can lead to many toddler eating problems and extreme fussiness. One benefit (among many others) of making your own food is that this allows you to introduce lumps very gradually.

Another benefit of introducing lumpy food is that the muscles used to chew are the same muscles used for speech, so chewing will help with your baby's speech development. Even if your baby doesn't have many teeth he can still chew using his gums.

Try thickening purées first of all, then adding lumps like really tiny pasta shapes, rice or couscous. Also try mashing a portion of your baby's food, then adding it to the purée, gradually increasing the ratio of mashed to puréed food. Try finely chopping a few of the vegetables so that her puréed meal contains tiny lumps, but keep these very soft for a while so her gums can squash them when she tries to chew. Well-cooked scrambled eggs are another good way of introducing texture. Offering finger foods at this age is a good idea as many babies learn to eat lumps this way rather than in purées and this is fine. Toast fingers, lightly steamed vegetable sticks, banana, tiny pieces of cheese (and later, sticks of cheese), grated apple, rice cakes, etc. are good finger foods.

The problem with organic jar baby foods is that they contain fewer natural vitamins and minerals than fresh foods. Studies have shown that babies fed on only organic baby food are at a higher risk of iron deficiency as no added iron is allowed in organic baby food. An infant fed exclusively on organic baby food would consume 20 per cent less iron than one eating non-organic baby food.

Feeding pre-term babies

Babies born before 37 weeks are considered pre-term and have a greater need for certain nutrients like iron and zinc, because these only start to be stored in your baby's body in the last weeks of pregnancy. Pre-term babies tend to be in a state of catch-up so make sure you give lots of nutrient-dense foods like cheese, avocado and potato.

Fruit

Going Bananas ☺ ☹

Babies love bananas and this recipe makes them taste truly scrumptious. It is delicious with vanilla ice cream. Try to use bananas with brown spots on the skin, as this shows they are ripe.

MAKES 1 PORTION
a knob of butter
1 small banana, peeled and sliced
a pinch of ground cinnamon
2 tablespoons freshly squeezed orange juice

Melt the butter in a small frying pan, stir in the sliced banana, sprinkle with a little cinnamon and sauté for 2 minutes. Pour in the orange juice and continue to cook for another 2 minutes. Mash with a fork.

Banana and Blueberry ☺ ☹

Bananas combine well with lots of different fruits. Try also peach, mango, dried apricot or prune. You can also mix banana and fruit combinations with some full-fat natural yoghurt. Serve straight away, before the banana turns brown.

MAKES 1 PORTION
25 g/1 oz blueberries
1 tablespoon water
1 small ripe banana, peeled and sliced

Put the blueberries into a saucepan with the water and cook for about 2 minutes or until the fruit just starts to burst open. Whiz with a hand blender, together with the sliced banana, until smooth.

Peach, Apple and Strawberry Purée ❄ ☺ ☺

You could also make Apple, Strawberry and Blueberry Purée using 25 g/ 1 oz blueberries instead of peach.

MAKES 2 PORTIONS
1 large apple, peeled, cored and chopped
1 large ripe peach, peeled, stoned and chopped
75 g/3 oz strawberries, halved
1 tablespoon baby rice

Steam the apple for about 4 minutes. Add the peach and strawberries to the steamer and continue to cook for about 3 minutes. Blend the fruits to a smooth purée and stir in the baby rice.

Apple, Apricot and Tofu ☺ ☺

Tofu is soya bean curd made from soya milk. It's a really good source of protein if you want to bring your child up on a vegetarian diet. It's also an excellent source of calcium, so adding tofu to fruit or vegetable purées is a good way to boost the calcium intake of babies who are allergic to cow's milk.

MAKES 2 PORTIONS
2 eating apples, peeled, cored and chopped
6 dried apricots, chopped
75 g/3 oz soft tofu

Place the apples and apricots in a pan and cover with water. Bring to the boil, reduce the heat, cover and simmer for about 5 minutes. Purée the fruit in a hand blender, together with the tofu.

Apricot, Apple and Peach Purée ❄ ☺ ☺

Dried apricots are a concentrated source of nutrients, they are rich in iron, potassium and betacarotene, and babies tend to like their sweet flavour.

MAKES 5 PORTIONS
75 g/3 oz ready-to-eat dried apricots
2 apples, peeled, cored and chopped
1 large ripe peach, skinned, stoned and chopped,
  or 1 ripe pear, peeled, cored and chopped

Put the apricots into a small saucepan and cover with water. Cook over a low heat for 5 minutes. Add the chopped apples and continue to cook for 5 minutes. Purée together with the peach or pear.

Yoghurt and Fruit ☺ ☺

It's important to make sure that as well as fruit and vegetables, your baby gets enough fat in his diet. Recipes like vegetables in cheese sauce and fruit mixes with yoghurt are very good for babies.

MAKES 1 PORTION
fresh fruit, e.g. 1 ripe peach, small mango or a combination
  like mango and banana
2 tablespoons full-fat natural yoghurt
a little maple syrup (optional)

Peel the fruit, remove any stones, mash the flesh and mix with the yoghurt. Stir in a little maple syrup to sweeten if necessary.

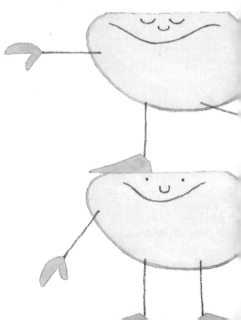

Vegetables

Lovely Lentils ❄ ☺ ☹

Lentils are a good cheap source of protein. They also provide iron, which is very important for brain development particularly between the ages of six months and two years. Lentils can be difficult for young babies to digest and should be combined with plenty of fresh vegetables as in this recipe. This tasty purée also makes a delicious soup for the family by simply adding more stock and some seasoning.

MAKES 8 PORTIONS

½ small onion, finely chopped
100 g/4 oz carrot, chopped
15 g/½ oz celery, chopped
1 tablespoon vegetable oil
50 g/2 oz split red lentils
200 g/7 oz sweet potato, peeled and chopped
400 ml/14 fl oz vegetable or chicken stock (see page 38 or 76) or water

Sauté the onion, carrot and celery in the vegetable oil for about 5 minutes or until softened. Add the lentils and sweet potato and pour over the stock or water. Bring to the boil, turn down the heat and simmer covered for 20 minutes. Purée in a blender.

Tomatoes and Carrots with Basil ❄ ☺ ☹

If you introduce your baby to new flavours at an early age, he will tend to grow up a less fussy eater.

MAKES 4 PORTIONS
125 g/4½ oz carrots, peeled and sliced
100 g/4 oz cauliflower, cut into florets
25 g/1 oz butter
200 g/7 oz ripe tomatoes, skinned, deseeded and roughly chopped
2–3 fresh basil leaves
50 g/2 oz Cheddar cheese, grated

Put the carrots in a small saucepan, cover with boiling water and simmer, covered, for 10 minutes. Add the cauliflower and cook, covered, for 7–8 minutes, adding extra water if necessary. Meanwhile, melt the butter, add the tomatoes and sauté until mushy. Stir in the basil and cheese until melted. Purée the carrots and cauliflower with about 3 tablespoons of the cooking liquid and the tomato sauce.

Baked Sweet Potato with Orange ❄ ☺ ☹

Sweet potatoes are delicious baked like jacket potatoes either in the oven or microwave and then combined with fruit like apple or peach purée. They are a good source of carbohydrate, vitamins and minerals.

MAKES 8 PORTIONS
1 medium sweet potato, scrubbed
2 tablespoons freshly squeezed orange juice
2 tablespoons milk

Cook the sweet potato on a baking sheet in an oven preheated to 200°C/400°F/Gas 6 for about 1 hour or until tender. Cool a little, then scoop out the flesh. Purée or mash with the orange juice and milk until smooth.

Sweet Potato with Spinach and Peas ❄ ☺ ☹

This purée makes a tasty introduction to spinach for your baby.

MAKES 5 PORTIONS
20 g/³/4 oz butter
50 g/2 oz leek, finely sliced
1 sweet potato (about 375 g/13 oz), peeled and chopped
200 ml/7 fl oz water
50 g/2 oz frozen peas
75 g/3 oz fresh baby spinach, washed and any tough stalks removed

Melt the butter in a saucepan and sauté the leek for 2–3 minutes or until softened. Add the sweet potato. Pour over the water, bring to the boil, then cover and simmer for 7–8 minutes. Add the peas and spinach and cook for 3 minutes. Purée the vegetables in a baby food grinder or blender to make a smooth consistency.

Sweet Vegetable Purée ❄ ☺ ☹

Peas and sweetcorn should be puréed in a mouli as the husks are indigestible.

MAKES 3 PORTIONS
25 g/1 oz chopped onion
75 g/3 oz carrot, peeled and chopped
1 tablespoon olive oil
150 g/5 oz potato, peeled and chopped
200 ml/7 fl oz water
2 tablespoons frozen sweetcorn
1 tablespoon frozen peas

Fry the onion and carrot gently in the oil for 5 minutes. Stir in the potato, add the water, bring to the boil, then cover and simmer for 10 minutes. Add the sweetcorn and peas and simmer for about 5 minutes. Purée in a mouli or baby food grinder.

Trio of Cauliflower, Red Pepper and Sweetcorn ❄ ☺ ☹

Babies like the bright colour and natural sweetness of these vegetables. Always purée sweetcorn in a mouli for young babies, to get rid of the tough outer skin.

MAKES 4 PORTIONS
100 g/4 oz cauliflower, broken into small florets
120 ml/4 fl oz milk
50 g/2 oz grated Cheddar cheese
25 g/1 oz sweet red pepper, chopped
75 g/3 oz frozen sweetcorn

Put the cauliflower in a small saucepan with the milk and cook over a low heat for about 8 minutes until tender. Stir in the grated cheese until melted. Meanwhile, steam the red pepper and sweetcorn or cook in some water in a small saucepan for about 6 minutes until tender. Drain the sweetcorn and pepper. Purée together with the cauliflower, milk and cheese in a mouli.

Cauliflower Cheese ❄ ☺ ☹

This is a great favourite with babies. Try using different cheeses or combinations of cheese until you find your baby's preferred taste. The cheese sauce can be used over a mixture of vegetables as well.

MAKES 5 PORTIONS
175 g/6 oz cauliflower

CHEESE SAUCE
15g/½ oz butter
1 tablespoon plain flour
150 ml/5 fl oz milk
50 g/2 oz Cheddar, Edam or Gruyère cheese, grated

Wash the cauliflower carefully, divide it into small florets and steam until tender (about 10 minutes). Meanwhile, for the sauce, melt the butter over a low heat in a heavy-bottomed saucepan and stir in the flour to make a smooth paste. Whisk in the milk and stir until thickened. Take the saucepan off the heat and stir in the grated cheese. Keep stirring until all the cheese has melted and the sauce is smooth.

Add the cauliflower to the sauce and purée in a blender for younger babies. For older babies, mash with a fork or chop into little pieces.

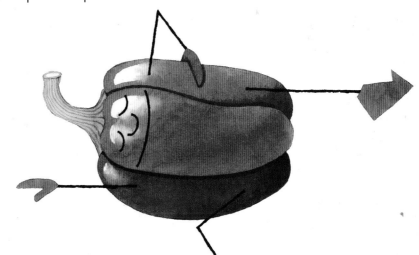

Courgette Gratin ❄ ☺ ☹

This creamy purée is also good using broccoli.

MAKES 6 PORTIONS
1 medium potato (about 100 g/4 oz), peeled and chopped
175 g/6 oz courgettes, sliced
a knob of butter
40 g/1½ oz Cheddar or Gruyère cheese
4 tablespoons milk

Boil the potato until soft. Steam the courgettes for 6–7 minutes. Drain the potatoes, add the butter and cheese and stir until melted. Purée the potato mixture, courgettes and milk with an electric hand blender or mash for older babies.

Leek and Potato Purée ❄ ☺ ☹

This was Lara's favourite vegetable purée. It also makes a delicious soup for adults if you add seasoning.

MAKES 4 PORTIONS
25 g/1 oz butter
125 g/4½ oz leeks, finely sliced
250 g/9 oz potatoes, peeled and chopped
300 ml/10 fl oz chicken or vegetable stock (see page 76 or 38)
2 tablespoons Greek yoghurt

Heat the butter in a saucepan. Add the leeks and cook over a low heat for 5 minutes, stirring occasionally. Add the potatoes and pour over the stock. Cover and cook for about 12 minutes or until tender. Strain the vegetables and purée in a mouli or blender, adding as much of the cooking liquid as necessary to make a smooth consistency. Stir in the yoghurt.

Courgette and Pea Souper ❄ ☺☹

When I experimented with this combination, the baby purée turned out to be so good that I also made a delicious soup for the rest of the family. Simply increase the quantities and add extra stock and seasoning.

MAKES 4 PORTIONS
½ small onion, peeled and finely chopped
15 g/½ oz butter
50 g/2 oz courgette, trimmed and thinly sliced
1 medium potato (about 150 g/5 oz), peeled and chopped
120 ml/4 fl oz chicken or vegetable stock (see page 76 or 38)
25 g/1 oz frozen peas

Sauté the onion in the butter until softened. Add the courgette, potato and stock. Bring to the boil, then cover and simmer for 12 minutes. Add the frozen peas, bring to the boil, then reduce the heat and continue to cook for 4–5 minutes. Purée in a blender.

Minestrone ❄ ☺ ☺

The vegetables in minestrone soup add texture but are nice and soft for your baby to chew. However, for younger babies you could blend this soup to the desired texture. Add a little seasoning and some extra stock to make this into a delicious soup for the rest of the family.

MAKES 4 ADULT PORTIONS OR 12 BABY PORTIONS
1 tablespoon vegetable oil
½ small onion, finely chopped
½ leek, white part only, washed and finely chopped
1 medium carrot, peeled and diced
½ celery stalk, diced
100 g/4 oz French beans, cut into 1 cm/½ inch lengths
1 potato, peeled and diced
1 tablespoon fresh parsley, finely chopped
2 teaspoons tomato purée
1.2 litres/2 pints chicken or vegetable stock (see pages 76 and 38)
3 tablespoons frozen peas
50 g/2 oz very small pasta shapes (see my own range of pasta shells, page 208)

Heat the oil in a saucepan and fry the onion and leek for 2 minutes, then add the carrot, celery, French beans, potato and parsley and sauté for 4 minutes. Stir in the tomato purée and cook for 1 minute. Pour over the chicken or vegetable stock and simmer, covered, for 20 minutes. Add the frozen peas and pasta and cook for 5 minutes (check the packet instructions for the cooking time of pasta).

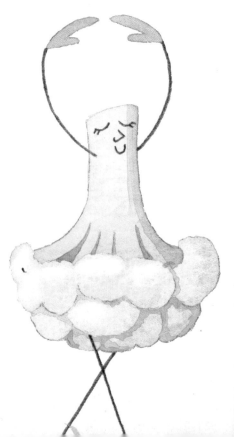

Fish

Tasty Fish with Cheese Sauce and Vegetables ❄ ☺ ☹

Fish and cheese sauce go really well together and the combination is always popular.

MAKES 6 PORTIONS

15 g/½ oz butter
60 g/2½ oz leeks, washed and finely sliced
1 medium carrot, peeled and chopped
60 g/2½ oz broccoli, cut into small florets
40 g/1½ oz frozen peas
150 g/5 oz cod fillets, skinned
150 ml/5 fl oz milk
3 peppercorns
1 bay leaf

CHEESE SAUCE

20 g/¾ oz butter
1 tablespoon plain flour
45 g/1¾ oz Cheddar cheese, grated

Melt the butter in a saucepan, add the leeks and sauté for 3 minutes. Add the carrot, cover with boiling water and cook for 12 minutes. Add the broccoli and cook for 5 minutes. Stir in the peas and simmer for 3–4 minutes or until the vegetables are tender.

Meanwhile, put the fish in a pan with the milk, peppercorns and bay leaf. Simmer for 4 minutes or until the fish is cooked. Strain, reserving the cooking liquid. Discard the peppercorns and bay leaf.

To prepare the sauce, melt the butter in a pan, stir in the flour and cook for 1 minute. Gradually whisk in the milk in which the fish was cooked. Bring to the boil and cook, stirring until the sauce has thickened. Remove from the heat, add the cheese and stir until melted.

Drain the vegetables and mix with the flaked fish and cheese sauce. Provided the vegetables are tender, this can be mashed or chopped for older babies who are starting to chew. Blend to a purée of the desired consistency for young babies.

Salmon with Carrots and Tomato ❄ ☺ ☹

This makes a good, creamy-textured fish purée.

MAKES 4 PORTIONS
225 g/8 oz carrots, peeled and sliced
150 g/5 oz salmon fillet
½ tablespoon milk (or enough to cover the salmon, see method below)
30 g/1 oz butter
2 ripe tomatoes, skinned, deseeded and chopped
40 g/1½ oz Cheddar cheese, grated

Put the carrots in a steamer set over a pan of boiling water and cook for 15–20 minutes or until tender. Meanwhile, place the fish in a microwave dish, add the milk, dot with half the butter and cover, leaving an air vent. Microwave on High for 1½–2 minutes. Alternatively, put the salmon in a pan, pour over enough milk to just cover, and simmer for about 4 minutes or until cooked.

Melt the remaining butter in a saucepan, add the tomatoes and sauté until softened and slightly mushy. Remove from the heat and stir in the cheese until melted. Blend the cooked carrots with the tomato mixture. Drain the cooking liquor from the fish, remove the skin and check there are no bones. Flake the fish and mix it with the carrots and tomatoes. For younger babies you can blend the fish together with the carrots and tomato for a smoother texture.

Oily fish like salmon provide the best source of essential fatty acids, which are very important for brain development – a baby's brain triples in size in the first year. A diet rich in EFAs can help children who have dyslexia, ADHD and dyspraxia. A lot of foods are now enriched with omega-3; however, most of these are plant-derived rather than fish oil-derived and are in quantities that provide little benefit. It is much better to concentrate on natural sources.

Plaice with Spinach and Cheese ❄ ☺ ☹

Frozen vegetables are a good alternative to fresh, and can often be more nutritious than vegetables that have been in the kitchen for several days. It also means you can make this when fresh spinach is not available.

MAKES 8 PORTIONS
225 g/8 oz plaice fillets, skinned
1 tablespoon milk
1 bay leaf
a few peppercorns
a knob of butter
175 g/6 oz fresh or 75 g/3 oz frozen spinach

CHEESE SAUCE
25 g/1 oz butter
2 tablespoons plain flour
175 ml/6 fl oz milk
50 g/2 oz Gruyère cheese

Put the plaice in a suitable dish with the milk, bay leaf, peppercorns and butter and microwave for about 3 minutes on High. Or, poach in a saucepan for 5 minutes. Meanwhile, cook the spinach in a saucepan with just a little water clinging to the leaves for about 3 minutes or cook frozen spinach following the packet instructions. Squeeze out the excess water. Make the cheese sauce (see page 67). Discard the bay leaf and peppercorns, flake the fish carefully and purée with the spinach and cheese sauce to the desired consistency.

Fillet of Cod with Sweet Potato ❄ ☺ ☹

The orange-fleshed sweet potato is an excellent source of betacarotene, which may help to prevent certain types of cancer.

MAKES 8 PORTIONS
225 g/8 oz sweet potato, peeled
75 g/3 oz cod, skinned and filleted
2 tablespoons milk
a knob of butter
juice of 1 orange (about 120 ml/4 fl oz)

Put the sweet potato into a saucepan, just cover with water, bring to the boil, then cover and simmer for 20 minutes or until soft. Put the fish in a suitable dish, add the milk, dot with butter, cover and microwave on High for 2 minutes or until the fish is cooked. Alternatively, poach the fish in a saucepan with the milk and butter for 6–7 minutes or until just cooked through. Put the cooked sweet potato, drained fish and orange juice into a blender and purée until smooth.

Fillet of Fish in an Orange Sauce ☺ ☹

Over the last 15 years this has been a very popular recipe – it has a lovely rich taste.

MAKES 5 PORTIONS
225 g/8 oz fillet of fish, skinned, e.g. cod, haddock or hake
juice of 1 orange (about 120 ml/4 fl oz)
40 g/1½ oz Cheddar cheese, grated
1 dessertspoon fresh parsley, finely chopped
25 g/1 oz crushed cornflakes
7 g/¼ oz margarine

Put the haddock in a greased dish, cover with the orange juice, cheese, parsley and cornflakes and dot with the margarine. Cover with foil and bake in an oven preheated to 180°C/350°F/Gas 4 for about 20 minutes. Alternatively, cover with a lid and cook in a microwave on High for 4 minutes.

Flake the fish carefully, removing any bones, and mash everything together with the liquid in which the fish was cooked.

Chicken

Chicken Stock and My First Chicken Purée ❄ ☺ ☹

Stock cubes are unsuitable for babies under a year as they are high in salt, so I make my own chicken stock and use it as a base for chicken and vegetable purées. It keeps in the fridge for 3 days. For babies over one year you can add 3 chicken stock cubes for a stronger flavour and you could also serve this as a soup with some noodles. Instead of a boiler chicken, you could use the carcass from a roast chicken.

MAKES APPROXIMATELY 2¼ LITRES/4 PINTS

1 large boiler chicken, plus giblets
2¼ litres/4 pints water
2 parsnips
3 large carrots
2 leeks
2 large onions
1 celery stalk
2 sprigs of fresh parsley
1 sachet bouquet garni

Cut the chicken into eight pieces, trimming off the excess fat. Trim, peel, wash and chop the vegetables as necessary. Put the chicken pieces into a large saucepan together with the giblets. Cover with the water, bring to the boil and skim the froth from the top. Add the remaining ingredients and simmer for about 3 hours. It is best to remove the chicken breasts after about 1½ hours if you are going to eat them; otherwise they will become too dry.

Leave the soup in the fridge overnight and remove any congealed fat from the top in the morning. Strain out all the chicken and vegetables to make the chicken stock.

You can purée some of the chicken breast in a mouli, together with a selection of the vegetables and some stock to make a chicken and vegetable purée. This also makes a wonderful clear chicken soup (with added stock cubes and seasoning) for older babies.

Chicken with Cottage Cheese ☺ ☺

Babies of this age are a little too young to eat pieces of chicken as finger food. This and the following three recipes show you simple ways of transforming cold chicken into tasty food for your baby.

MAKES 2 PORTIONS
50 g/2 oz cooked boneless chicken, chopped
1 tablespoon natural yoghurt
1½ tablespoons cottage cheese with pineapple

Mix together the chicken, yoghurt and cottage cheese. Blend to the desired consistency.

Chicken Salad Purée ❄ ☺ ☺

What could be simpler? For toddlers, simply chop the ingredients, leave out the yoghurt and mix with mayonnaise or salad cream.

MAKES 1 PORTION
25 g/1 oz cooked boneless chicken
1 slice cucumber, peeled and chopped
1 small tomato, skinned, deseeded and chopped
50 g/2 oz avocado, peeled and chopped
1 tablespoon mild natural yoghurt

Put all the ingredients into a blender and purée until the desired consistency. Serve immediately.

Chicken with Sweet Potato and Apple ❄ ☺ ☹

This combination gives a smooth texture and sweet taste that babies like.

MAKES 4 PORTIONS
15 g/½ oz butter
40 g/1½ oz onion, chopped
100 g/4 oz chicken breast, chopped
½ eating apple, peeled and chopped
1 sweet potato (about 300 g/11 oz), peeled and chopped
200 ml/7 fl oz chicken stock (see page 76)

Melt the butter in a saucepan, add the onion and sauté for 2–3 minutes. Add the chicken and sauté until it turns opaque. Add the apple, sweet potato and stock. Bring to the boil, cover and simmer for 15 minutes. Purée to the desired consistency.

Easy One-Pot Chicken ❄ ☺ ☹

This is an ideal purée for introducing young babies to chicken.

MAKES 12 PORTIONS
½ small onion, peeled and chopped
15 g/½ oz butter
100 g/4 oz chicken breast, cut into chunks
1 medium carrot, peeled and sliced
275 g/10 oz sweet potato, peeled and chopped
300 ml/10 fl oz chicken stock (see page 76)

Sauté the onion in the butter until softened. Add the chicken breast and sauté for 3–4 minutes. Add the vegetables, pour over the stock, bring to the boil and simmer, covered, for about 30 minutes or until the chicken is cooked through and the vegetables are tender. Purée in a blender to the desired consistency.

Chicken in Tomato Sauce ❄ ☺ ☹

MAKES 12 PORTIONS
25 g/1 oz chopped onion
100 g/4 oz carrot, thinly sliced
1½ tablespoons vegetable oil
1 small chicken breast, cut into chunks
100 g/4 oz potato, peeled and chopped
200 g/7 oz canned chopped tomatoes
150 ml/5 fl oz chicken stock (see page 76)

Sauté the onion and carrot in the vegetable oil until softened, then add the chicken and potato and continue to cook for 3 minutes. Pour over the chopped tomatoes together with the chicken stock. Bring to the boil and cook over a low heat for about 30 minutes or until the potato is quite soft. Put the mixture through a mouli or, for babies of nine months and older, chop in a blender. You could also add a little milk to make a smoother texture if you wish.

Fruity Chicken with Apricots ❄ ☺ ☹

Babies like the combination of chicken and fruit. Dried apricots are one of nature's great health foods. They are a good source of betacarotene, iron and potassium and the drying process increases their concentration. They also make great finger food. This is good by itself or you can mix it with 4 tablespoons of cooked rice or pasta.

MAKES 3 PORTIONS
2 teaspoons light olive oil
½ small onion, chopped (approx. 50 g/2 oz)
1 small garlic clove, crushed
75 g/3 oz chicken breast, cut into pieces
3 dried apricots, chopped
150 ml/5 fl oz passata (sieved tomatoes)
150 ml/5 fl oz chicken stock (see page 76) or water

Heat the oil in a pan and sauté the onion for about 5 minutes or until softened. Add the garlic and cook for 1 minute. Add the chicken and sauté for 2–3 minutes until sealed. Add the apricots, passata and stock or water. Bring to the boil then cover and simmer for about 5 minutes.

Red meats

Braised Beef with Sweet Potato ❄ ☺ ☹

Both this and the recipe below make good introductions to red meat.

MAKES 6 PORTIONS

20 g/³/4 oz butter or margarine
1 leek, washed and sliced (approx. 150 g/5 oz)
125 g/4½ oz braising steak, cut into cubes
1 tablespoon flour
100 g/4 oz button mushrooms, sliced
275 g/10 oz sweet potato, peeled and chopped
250 ml/8 fl oz chicken stock (see page 76)
juice of 1 orange (about 120 ml/4 fl oz)

Melt the butter or margarine in a flameproof casserole and sauté the leek for about 4 minutes until softened. Roll the meat in the flour, add to the leek and sauté until browned. Add the mushrooms and and sauté for 1 minute. Add the sweet potato, stock and orange juice. Bring to the boil and transfer to an oven preheated to 180°C/350°F/Gas 4 for 1¼ hours or until the meat is tender. Blend to the desired consistency using as much of the cooking liquid as necessary.

Liver Special ❄ ☺ ☹

MAKES 6 PORTIONS

75 g/3 oz calf's liver, or 2 chicken livers
120 ml/4 fl oz chicken stock (see page 76)
25 g/1 oz leek, white part only, chopped
25 g/1 oz mushrooms, chopped
50 g/2 oz carrot, peeled and chopped
1 potato, peeled and chopped
a knob of butter
½ tablespoon milk

Trim and chop the liver and cook in the stock with the leek, mushrooms and carrot for about 8 minutes over a low heat. Boil the potato until tender and mash with the butter and milk. Purée the liver and vegetables and mix with the potato.

Pasta

Tomato and Courgette Pasta Stars ❄ ☺ ☹

This tasty pasta sauce takes only about 10 minutes to prepare.

MAKES 3 PORTIONS
25 g/1 oz pasta stars, uncooked
75 g/3 oz courgette, trimmed and diced
25 g/1 oz butter
3 medium tomatoes (about 200 g/7 oz), skinned, deseeded and chopped
25 g/1 oz Cheddar cheese, grated

Cook the pasta according to the packet instructions, or longer for young babies. Sauté the courgette in the butter for about 5 minutes. Add the tomatoes and cook over a low heat for 5 minutes. Remove from the heat and stir in the cheese until melted. Purée in a blender and stir in the pasta.

Vegetable and Cheese Pasta Sauce ❄ ☺ ☹

MAKES 3 PORTIONS OF SAUCE
65 g/2½ oz carrot, peeled and sliced
40 g/1½ oz broccoli florets
25 g/1 oz butter
2 tablespoons plain flour
175 ml/6 fl oz milk
40 g/1½ oz grated Cheddar cheese

Steam the carrot for 10 minutes, then add the broccoli florets and cook for 7 minutes more. Meanwhile, melt the butter in a small saucepan and stir in the flour to make a thick paste. Gradually add the milk, bring to the boil and stir continuously until the sauce thickens. Simmer for 1 minute. Remove from the heat and stir in the grated cheese. Add the cooked vegetables to the cheese sauce and blend to a purée. Serve with tiny cooked pasta shapes.

My First Bolognese Sauce ❄ ☺ ☹

MAKES 3 PORTIONS

1 tablespoon olive oil
1 small onion, peeled and chopped
1 garlic clove, crushed
1 medium carrot, peeled and grated
½ celery stalk, finely chopped
100 g/4 oz lean minced beef
3 medium tomatoes, skinned and chopped
½ teaspoon tomato purée
150 ml/5 fl oz unsalted chicken stock
3 tablespoons tiny pasta shapes

Heat the oil and sauté the onion, garlic, carrot and celery for 5 minutes. Add the minced beef and sauté until browned, stirring occasionally. Stir in the tomatoes, tomato purée and chicken stock. Bring to the boil, then simmer for 15 minutes. Meanwhile, cook the pasta shapes according to the packet instructions. Transfer the sauce to a blender and purée to a fairly smooth consistency. Drain the pasta and mix with the sauce.

Tomato and Basil Pasta Sauce ❄ ☺ ☹

Butterfly-shaped pasta is fun for babies to grasp in their hands.

MAKES 2 PORTIONS OF SAUCE

15 g/½ oz butter
2 tablespoons chopped onion
150 g/5 oz ripe tomatoes, skinned, deseeded and chopped
2 fresh basil leaves, torn
2 teaspoons cream cheese

Melt the butter in a saucepan and sauté the onion until softened. Add the tomatoes and sauté for 3 minutes or until mushy. Stir in the basil and cream cheese and heat through. Purée in a blender.

Napolitana Pasta Sauce ❄ ☺ ☹

A tasty tomato sauce which goes well with all types of pasta – my children love this with ravioli stuffed with ricotta and spinach.

MAKES 4 PORTIONS OF SAUCE
1 tablespoon olive oil
½ small onion, peeled and chopped
½ garlic clove, peeled and crushed
50 g/2 oz carrot, peeled and chopped
200 ml/7 fl oz passata
3 tablespoons water
2 fresh basil leaves, roughly torn
1 teaspoon grated Parmesan cheese
1 teaspoon cream cheese

Heat the olive oil and sauté the onion, garlic and carrot for 6 minutes. Add the passata, water, basil and Parmesan. Cover and simmer for 15 minutes. Purée the sauce and stir in the cream cheese. Mix with pasta and serve.

Popeye Pasta ❄ ☺ ☹

MAKES 4 PORTIONS
100 g/4 oz frozen or 225 g/8 oz fresh spinach, washed
40 g (1½ oz) tiny pasta stars
15 g/½ oz butter
2 tablespoons milk
2 tablespoons cream cheese
40 g/1½ oz Gruyère cheese, grated

Cook the spinach according to the packet instructions or, if fresh, with just the water clinging to its leaves in a microwave or in a saucepan over a low heat until tender. Press out the excess water. Cook the pasta according to the packet instructions. Meanwhile, melt the butter in a small frying pan and sauté the cooked spinach. Combine the spinach with the milk and cheeses, and chop finely in a food processor. Mix with the cooked pasta.

Second-stage weaning meal planner

	Breakfast	Mid-morning	Lunch	Mid-afternoon	Tea	Bedtime
Day 1	Weetabix with milk Mashed banana Milk	Milk	Chicken with Sweet Potato and Apple Fruit* Juice	Milk	Leek and Potato Purée Apricot, Apple and Peach Purée Water or juice	Milk
Day 2	Ready Brek or porridge with milk Fruit purée Milk	Milk	Salmon with Carrots and Tomato Mashed banana Juice	Milk	Courgette and Pea Souper Yoghurt Water or juice	Milk
Day 3	Apple purée and baby cereal Toast Milk	Milk	Cauliflower Cheese Fruit Juice	Milk	Braised Beef with Sweet Potato Rusk Water or juice	Milk
Day 4	Baby cereal with milk Banana and Blueberry Fromage frais Milk	Milk	Lovely Lentils Peaches and Rice Juice	Milk	Minestrone Toast Water or juice	Milk

* Your baby should be able to hold and eat soft pieces of fruit

	Breakfast	Mid-morning	Lunch	Mid-afternoon	Tea	Bedtime
Day 5	Weetabix with milk **Peach, Apple and Strawberry Purée** Milk	Milk	Pasta with **Vegetable and Cheese Pasta Sauce** **Going Bananas** Juice	Milk	**My First Bolognese Sauce** Pear purée Water or juice	Milk
Day 6	Baby cereal with milk **Peach, Apple and Strawberry Purée** Milk	Milk	**Tomatoes and Carrots with Basil** Fruit Juice	Milk	**Fillet of Fish in an Orange Sauce** Fruit Water	Milk
Day 7	Ready Brek with milk **Yoghurt and Fruit** Milk	Milk	**Sweet Potato with Spinach and Peas** **Apricot, Apple and Peach Purée** Juice	Milk	**Easy One-Pot Chicken** **Apricot, Apple and Peach Purée** Water or juice	Milk

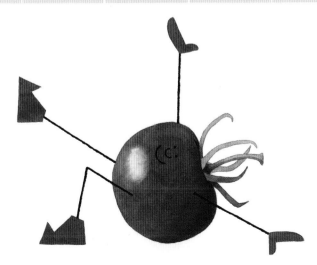

CHAPTER FOUR

Nine to twelve months

Towards the end of the first year, a baby's weight gain usually slows down quite dramatically. Often babies who have been good eaters in the past become much more difficult to feed. Try to give your baby his meals in a high-chair at the table. Try to eat together, and make mealtimes fun and sociable. If he can see everyone around him eating happily, it is likely that he will want to join in.

This can be a difficult stage for many parents – babies find it hard to cope with more lumpy food and generally prefer to feed themselves than be fed, though their aim is often far from perfect. Interestingly, while many babies refuse anything with lumps in it, they will happily chew on finger foods like carrot or cucumber sticks, or pieces of fruit. Try nutritious finger foods like Chicken and Apple Balls (page 122), Salmon Footballs (page 108) or Fresh Fruit Ice Lollies (page 120) – good for soothing sore gums.

Mealtime Patience

Let your baby experiment by allowing her to use a spoon. Most of the food will probably end up on you or on the floor, but the more you allow your baby to experiment, the quicker she will master the art of feeding herself. Put a plastic splash mat under the high chair to catch the food that falls on the floor so that you can recycle it. It is probably best to have two bowls of food and two spoons; one which you use to spoon-feed your baby, the other (preferably a bowl which sticks to the table by suction) for your baby to play with. You will need lots of patience at mealtimes, as many babies are very easily distracted at this stage and prefer to play with their food rather than eat it. If all else fails, I find that if you can attract their attention by giving them a small toy to hold, you can sometimes slip food into their mouths on a spoon and they will eat without really noticing what they are doing and forget to put up any resistance!

Toddlers often go into 'meltdown' just before dinner, especially if there has been some delay. Just before 'meltdown' is a good time to offer some cut-up vegetables like carrots, cucumber or peppers. If they haven't been snacking they will be hungry and therefore more likely to eat them, and if they do get full, they will be full on vegetables, which is great. Just because a child doesn't like cooked vegetables doesn't mean they won't like the same vegetable raw, so always try both versions. Rather than chopping the vegetables and fruit into small pieces, I find that sometimes children prefer to be given a whole carrot or a chunk of cucumber.

Continue giving breast or formula milk as your baby's main drink. Cow's milk is not suitable as a main drink because it is low in essential vitamins and minerals like iron. However, as solid-food intake increases, milk need no longer form such a staple part of your child's diet, although they should still be drinking about 500 ml/18 fl oz of milk a day (or the equivalent as dairy products or in cooking). It is an important source of protein and calcium. Many mothers assume that when their baby cries it is because she wants more milk, but often babies of this age are given too much milk and not enough solid food. If you fill your baby's stomach with milk when she really wants some solid food, you will not get a very satisfied baby.

Whilst it is a good idea to switch off the TV and try to provide a calm atmosphere, there is no doubt that there are some babies who will eat much better with the gentle distraction of a simple (washable) toy at the high-chair. Some babies are much easier to feed if their hands are occupied so giving your baby a spoon to hold is also worth a try . . .

If you have a juice extractor, you can make all sorts of wonderful fruit and vegetable drinks for your baby – try combinations like apple, strawberry and banana. Your baby should now be drinking happily from a cup, the bottle kept for her bedtime drink of warm milk. Your baby will be teething at this age and very often sore gums can put her off eating for a while. Don't worry, as she will make up for this later that day or the next day. (Rubbing a teething gel on your baby's gums, or giving her something very cold to chew, can help relieve soreness and restore appetite.)

It is a good idea to eat something with your baby at mealtimes. There are some mothers who sit opposite their babies and try to spoon food into their mouths whilst eating nothing themselves. Babies are great mimics and will be much more likely to enjoy eating if they see you tucking in as well.

When learning to feed themselves, babies should be allowed to smear food and generally make a mess.

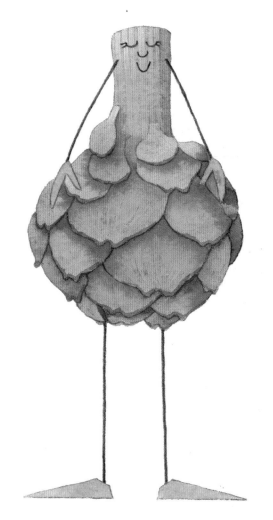

Make mealtimes a positive experience. Many babies hate having their faces wiped, so only wipe at the end of a meal unless they get themselves into a real mess. Try to wipe their face or hands with a flannel and warm water rather than baby wipes as the alcohol can sting any little sore areas on their chins from teething.

The Foods to Choose

Now you can be a little more adventurous with the food that you make for your baby. It is a good idea to develop her tastes for garlic and herbs, both of which are very healthy. Children tend to be less fussy eaters if they are introduced to a wide range of foods early. Again, if your baby dislikes certain foods, never force her to eat them; just leave out those foods and perhaps reintroduce them in a couple of days' time. Try also to vary the foods as much as possible, as this will lead to a more balanced diet. If you give your child a favourite food too often, it is possible she will go off it altogether.

Your baby can now eat berry fruits (these can be sieved to get rid of the indigestible seeds). Fruit jellies will be interesting for your baby to look at, feel and eat. Your baby should also like fruit and vegetables that have been grated.

Oily fish like salmon, sardines and fresh tuna should be included in your baby's diet as they contain essential fatty acids and iron that are important for the brain and visual development. Fish is quite simple to cook and if you use my recipes it is easy to make it appealing to your baby. All fish must obviously be very fresh.

When possible, try to make your baby's food look attractive on the plate. Choose colourful fruit and vegetables and make shapes like little faces. Don't pile too much food onto the plate and use mini-ramekin dishes to make individual portions of shepherd's pie or fish pie (you can also freeze them).

Meat

Red meat is good for young children as it provides the best source of iron. If using fresh mince choose good-quality meat and ask your butcher to mince it for you rather than buying it ready prepared. After cooking mince for young babies, I find that if I chop it in a food processor for 30 seconds, it becomes softer and easier to chew. At this age it is good to mix meat with tiny pasta shapes or rice. It is best not to give sausages or other processed meats to children, like pâté or meat pies. The cocktail meatballs on page 180 would make excellent finger food.

Textures and quantities

It is easy to get into the habit of only giving your baby soft foods, but you should try to vary the consistency of the food you offer. There is no need to purée all foods. Babies do not need teeth to be able to chew; gums do a great job on foods that are not too hard. Give some food mashed (fish), some grated (cheese), some diced (carrots) and some whole (pieces of chicken, slices of toast and pieces of raw fruit).

As far as quantities are concerned, you must let your baby's appetite be your guide. You can start to freeze food in larger plastic containers and freeze individual portions like mini shepherd's pies in small ramekin dishes. Many meals in this chapter can be enjoyed by the whole family, in which case adult-sized portions are given.

Finger foods

By the age of nine months, your baby will probably want to start feeding herself. It is a good idea, therefore, to start giving her some foods that are easy to eat with her fingers. Finger foods are great for occupying your child while you prepare her meal – or you could make a whole meal of finger foods.

Never leave your child unattended whilst eating.

It is very easy for a baby to choke on even very small pieces of food. Avoid giving your baby whole nuts, fruits that contain stones, whole grapes, ice cubes, olives or any other foods that might get stuck in her throat.

What To Do If Your Baby Chokes

If your baby chokes, lay her face down on your forearm or lap with her head lower than her chest. Support her head and give her five light slaps between her shoulders with your free hand.

Fruit and Ice Lollies

When giving your baby fruit, make sure any pips or stones have been removed. If she finds it difficult to chew, give soft fruits that melt in the mouth such as bananas, peaches or grated fruits. Berry and citrus fruits should only be given in small quantities to start with. Remove as much pith as possible.

Many babies who are teething really enjoy biting into something cold as this soothes sore gums. Try making fresh fruit ice lollies: fill lolly moulds with tasty combinations of pureed fruit, fruit juices, smoothies and yoghurt (see page 208 for my own range of lolly moulds).

Dried Fruits

These are a good source of fibre, iron and energy. Choose ready-to-eat fruits that are soft. Some dried apricots are treated with sulphur dioxide to preserve their bright orange colour; these should be avoided as they can trigger an asthma attack in susceptible babies. Don't give your baby lots of dried fruit as it can be difficult to digest – and laxative.

Fruity ideas

Apple, apricot, avocado, banana, blueberries, cherries, clementine, grapes, kiwi fruit, mango, melon, nectarine, orange, papaya, peach, pear, plum, raspberries, strawberries, tomato

More fruity ideas

Apple rings, dried apricots, banana chips, dates, dried pears, prunes, raisins, sultanas

Vegetables

To begin with, give your baby soft cooked vegetables cut into pieces that are easy for her to hold, and encourage her to bite off little pieces. (It is best to steam vegetables as this will help to preserve Vitamin C.) Gradually cook the vegetables for less time so that your baby gets used to having to chew harder. Once your baby has good coordination, she will enjoy picking up little vegetables like peas and sweetcorn.

When your baby has mastered the art of feeding herself cooked vegetables, you can introduce raw vegetables. Even if your baby is unable to bite into these sticks, she will enjoy chewing on them as an aid to teething. In fact, sticks of raw vegetables such as carrots and cucumber are very soothing for sore gums if they are chilled in the freezer or in iced water for a few minutes. Large pieces of raw vegetables are safer than small pieces as a baby will nibble off what she can manage, whereas a small piece put into her mouth whole could cause her to choke if she tried to swallow it.

Once your baby can chew well, try giving her corn on the cob. Cut the corn in half or into three pieces or look out for little mini-sized corn cobs in some supermarkets – just right for babies. Corn is fun to eat and babies love to hold and chew it. Vegetables are also very good when dipped into sauces and purées. Try using some of the recipes for vegetable purées as dipping sauces.

Keep a supply of puréed vegetables in the freezer, stored in ice cube trays. Include favourites like butternut squash, sweet potato and carrot and pea and some that your child may not be so keen on like courgette, spinach or broccoli. Defrost the amount you need and add them to popular dishes.
- Mix them with pasta sauce and tiny pasta shapes
- Hide in cheesy mashed potato
- Use as a spread in toasted cheese sandwiches.

Breads and Rusks

Pieces of toast, rusks and firm bread, like pitta bread and bagels, make good finger food and can be dipped into purées and sauces. Rice cakes come in lots of different flavours and are excellent for teething, as they seem to hold together well. You can also make grilled cheese on toast or spread toast with no-sugar conserves.

Many baby rusks on the market contain as much sugar as a sweet biscuit and even so-called low-sugar rusks can contain more than 15 per cent sugar. It is very easy to make your own sugar-free alternative from wholemeal bread (see below).

Vegetable finger food

Broccoli, carrots, cauliflower, celery, corn on the cob, courgettes, mushrooms, new potatoes, sweet potato

Home-made rusks

For home-made savoury rusks, simply cut a thick (1 cm/½ inch) slice of wholemeal (granary or rye) bread into three strips. Melt ⅛ teaspoon Marmite in 1 teaspoon boiling water, and brush this evenly over the bread strips. Bake in an oven preheated to 180°C/350°F/Gas 4 for 15 minutes. Leave out the Marmite if your baby prefers and add a little grated cheese. You can prepare a store of rusks in advance and keep them in an airtight container for 3–4 days.

Miniature sandwiches

Little sandwiches cut into fingers, squares, small triangles or even animal shapes using a biscuit cutter are very popular with babies. Some suggestions for sandwich fillings are given below; use your imagination to come up with original, tasty combinations.

Filling suggestions

mashed banana and/or peanut butter, tuna with sweetcorn and mayonnaise, hummus, cottage cheese with pineapple, cream cheese with strawberry jam or chopped dried apricots, grated cheese and tomato, mashed sardines with tomato ketchup, egg mayonnaise and salad cress

Breakfast Cereals

Babies love to pick up and eat little pieces of breakfast cereal like Cheerios. Try to choose cereals that are fortified with iron and vitamins and which do not have added sugar. Again, some suggestions are given below.

Cheese

Start by giving your baby grated cheese or cut wafer-thin slices. Once she has mastered chewing, you can move on to chunks and strips of cheese. I have found that the following cheeses are especially popular: Cheddar, mozzarella, Edam, Gouda, Emmenthal and Gruyère. Cream cheese and cottage cheeses are also favourites. Keep away from strong cheeses like blue cheese, Brie and Camembert. Always make sure that the cheese you give your baby is pasteurised.

Good morning munchies

Cheerios, cornflakes, granola, Shreddies

Pasta

Pasta comes in all shapes and sizes, including tiny stars, mini shells, and animal and alphabet shapes (see my own range on page 208). I have given some recipes for pasta sauces but most of the vegetable purées can also be served with pasta. You can try tossing pasta in melted butter and sprinkling with grated cheese. This is usually a great favourite, even with the fussy eaters.

Chicken

Slices or chunks of cooked chicken (or turkey) make great finger food. Give the dark meat as well as the white as it contains twice as much zinc and iron. Bang Bang Chicken and Chicken with Cornflakes (see page 124) are particularly good given as finger food.

Fish

Pieces of flaked white fish are good as they are low in fat, high in protein and easy for your child to chew. You can give them to your baby either plain or mixed with a sauce. Make your own fish fingers by cutting white fish fillets into strips, coating in flour, beaten egg and crushed cornflakes, and then frying until golden. You could also try the Salmon Footballs on page 120. Do take extra care when serving fish to your baby in any recipe to check the fish thoroughly for bones before you cook it and when flaking it. Make sure you include some oily fish like salmon or sardines in your child's diet, preferably twice a week.

Breakfast

The first meal of the day is important for all of us after a night's fasting, particularly so for energetic babies and toddlers!

For this age group recipes can now contain more interesting and more healthy grains. Wheat-germ is particularly good and can be sprinkled onto cereals or yoghurt. Mixing cereals and fruit makes a delicious and nutritious start to the day. Many of the home-made cereals can be mixed with apple juice instead of milk.

Cheese is important for strong bones and teeth. You can offer cheese on toast or little strips for your baby to hold. Eggs are an excellent source of protein, vitamins and iron. Give your baby scrambled eggs or an omelette but make sure that the white and yolk are cooked until solid. Fresh fruit provides vitamins, minerals and substances called phytochemicals which help prevent cancer. Give fruit as finger foods, make fruit salads or offer stewed fruit, such as apple or rhubarb.

Highly refined, sugar-coated cereals should be avoided. Do not be fooled by the list of added vitamins on the side of the packet – unprocessed cereals are much healthier for your child. Wholegrain cereals are also a good source of iron, but you will need to include some vitamin C such as diluted orange juice or strawberries in order for your baby to absorb the iron.

Breakfast

Fruity Swiss Muesli ☺ ☹

This tasty and nutritious breakfast will make a good start to the day for the whole family. You can vary the fruit in the muesli, adding, for example, peaches, strawberries, bananas or ready-to-eat dried apricots.

MAKES 4 CHILD OR 2 ADULT PORTIONS
65 g/2½ oz rolled oats
15 g/½ oz wheat germ
175 ml/6 fl oz apple juice
1 teaspoon lemon juice
1 apple, peeled and grated
1 pear, peeled, cored and chopped
1 tablespoon maple syrup
120–150 ml/4–5 fl oz natural yoghurt

Combine the rolled oats, wheat germ and apple juice. Set aside for a couple of hours or refrigerate overnight. Next morning, mix the lemon juice with the grated apple and stir this into the oat mixture together with the chopped pear, maple syrup and yoghurt.

Fruity Yoghurt ☺ ☹

Many commercial fruit yoghurts have a lot of added sugar. It is easy to make your own, adding a combination of your baby's favourite foods.

MAKES 2 PORTIONS
½ ripe peach stoned, skinned and chopped
½ small banana, peeled and chopped
150 ml/5 fl oz natural yoghurt
2 teaspoons maple syrup

Simply mix all the ingredients together and serve. Mash the fruit for younger babies.

My Favourite Pancakes ❄ ☺ ☹

Pancakes for breakfast are a treat, and this simple recipe is foolproof. Pancakes can be made in advance, refrigerated and reheated. To freeze, interleave with non-stick baking paper. Serve with maple syrup and fresh fruit.

MAKES 12 PANCAKES
100 g/4 oz plain flour
generous pinch of salt
2 eggs
300 ml/10 fl oz milk
50 g/2 oz melted butter

Sift the flour and salt into a mixing bowl, make a well in the centre and add the eggs. Use a balloon whisk to incorporate the eggs into the flour and gradually whisk in the milk until just smooth.

Brush a heavy-based 15–18 cm/6–7 inch frying pan with the melted butter and when hot, pour in about 2 tablespoons of the batter. Quickly tilt the pan from side to side to form a thin layer of batter and cook for 1 minute. Flip the pancake over with a spatula and cook until the underside is slightly golden. Continue with the rest of the batter, brushing the pan with melted butter when necessary.

Apricot, Apple and Pear Custard ❄ ☺ ☹

Dried apricots are one of nature's great health foods. They are a good concentrated source of betacarotene, potassium and iron. This tasty fruit purée works well for breakfast or dessert.

MAKES 3 PORTIONS
75 g/3 oz ready-to-eat dried apricots
1 large eating apple, peeled, cored and chopped
1 tablespoon custard powder
150 ml/5 fl oz milk
1 ripe pear, peeled, cored and chopped

Gently heat the apricots and apple in a small saucepan with 4 tablespoons of water for 8–10 minutes or until soft. In a saucepan, blend the custard powder with a little of the milk to make a smooth paste. Then add the remaining milk and slowly bring to the boil, stirring until thickened and smooth. Blend the cooked fruit and pear to the desired consistency and stir in the custard.

A Grown-Up Breakfast ☺ ☹

Unfortunately many of the breakfast cereals designed specifically for children are laden with sugar. I prefer to give my children some of the more old-fashioned cereals like Weetabix, Ready Brek, porridge or muesli and sweeten these with fresh fruit.

MAKES 1 PORTION
½ Weetabix
1 small banana
3 tablespoons mild natural yoghurt or milk

Finely crumble the Weetabix and mash the banana. Combine all the ingredients together and serve.

Summer Fruit Muesli ☺ ☹

Simply soak the oats overnight and stir in extra fresh fruits like peaches or strawberries the next day for a tasty nutritious muesli. If your baby is too young for lumpy food, this can be blended to a fine purée.

MAKES 4 ADULT PORTIONS
100 g/4 oz porridge oats
2 tablespoons sultanas or raisins
300 ml/10 fl oz apple and mango juice
2 eating apples, peeled, cored and grated
4–6 tablespoons milk
a little maple syrup or honey (for babies over 1 year)

Mix the oats, sultanas and apple and mango juice in a bowl, cover and leave to soak overnight in the fridge. In the morning stir in the remaining ingredients and any extra fruit and drizzle over a little maple syrup or honey (if using).

Banana and Prune Fool ☺ ☹

This only takes a couple of minutes to prepare and it is very tasty. It is also a good recipe to try if your baby is a little bit constipated.

MAKES 1 PORTION
5 canned prunes in fruit juice, stoned
1 small ripe banana, peeled
1 tablespoon natural yoghurt
1 tablespoon cream cheese

Whiz the prunes, banana, yoghurt and cream cheese together in a blender with 1–2 tablespoons of the juice from the canned fruit.

The Three Bears' Breakfast ☺ ☹

This makes a very nutritious breakfast, but make sure your child gobbles it up before Goldilocks comes to the front door!

MAKES 2 ADULT PORTIONS
300 ml/10 fl oz milk
40 g/1½ oz porridge oats
25 g/1 oz ready-to-eat dried peaches or apricots, chopped
1 teaspoon chopped raisins

Pour the milk into a saucepan and bring to the boil. Mix in the oats and bring back to the boil, stirring. Add the chopped dried fruit, lower the heat and simmer for about 4 minutes or until thickened.

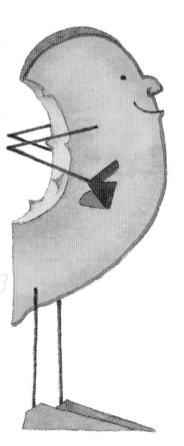

Matzo Brei ☺ ☹

For those of you who have never heard of matzo, it is a large square of unleavened bread similar to crispbread. When uncooked, it is very brittle and my son Nicholas loved to snap it into pieces and strew it all over the floor. This is why I prefer to serve it cooked!

MAKES 2 ADULT PORTIONS
2 matzos
1 egg, beaten
25 g/1 oz butter
a little caster sugar (optional)

Break the matzos into bite-sized pieces and soak for a couple of minutes in cold water. Squeeze out the excess water, then add the matzos to the beaten egg. Melt the butter in a frying pan until sizzling and fry the matzos on both sides. Sprinkle with sugar if wished.

French Toast Cut-Outs ☺ ☹

It's fun sometimes to cut the bread into a variety of animal shapes using biscuit cutters. For a treat, serve with maple syrup or jam.

MAKES 2 PORTIONS

1 egg
2 tablespoons milk
a pinch of ground cinnamon (optional)
2 slices white or raisin bread
25 g/1 oz butter

Beat the egg lightly with the milk and cinnamon, if using, and pour into a shallow dish. Dip the bread in this mixture, coating each side. Melt the butter and fry the slices or animal shapes until golden on both sides.

Cheese Scramble ☺ ☹

Until your child is one year, scrambled egg should be cooked until it is quite firm and not runny. You could use cottage cheese instead of Cheddar.

MAKES 1 PORTION

1 egg
1 tablespoon milk
15 g/½ oz butter
1 tablespoon Cheddar cheese, finely grated
1 tomato, skinned and deseeded

Beat the egg with the milk. Melt the butter over a low heat, then add the egg mixture. Cook slowly, stirring all the time. When the mixture has thickened and looks soft and creamily set, add the cheese and chopped tomato. Serve immediately.

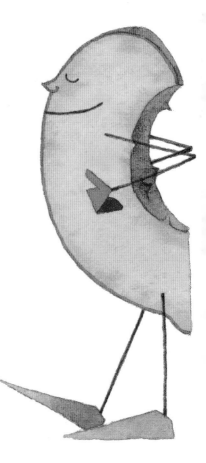

Fruit

Baked Apples with Raisins ☺ ☹

Cooking apples have a better flavour, but eating apples are sweeter. You can use either for this recipe. The apples are delicious served with ice cream or custard.

MAKES 6 BABY OR 2 ADULT PORTIONS

2 apples
120 ml/4 fl oz apple juice or water
2 tablespoons raisins
a little ground cinnamon
1 tablespoon honey or maple syrup
(if using cooking apples)
a little butter or margarine

Core the apples and prick the skins with a fork to stop them bursting. Put the apples in an ovenproof dish and pour the apple juice or water around the base. Put 1 tablespoon of the raisins into the centre of each apple, sprinkle with cinnamon and (if using cooking apples) pour over honey or maple syrup. Top each with a little butter. Bake in an oven preheated to 180°C/350°F/Gas 4 for about 45 minutes.

For young babies, scoop out the pulp of the apple and purée roughly with the raisins and some of the juices from the dish.

Apple and Blackberry ❄ ☺ ☹

Blackberries and apples make a delicious combination, and the blackberries (which are rich in Vitamin C) turn the apples a wonderful purple colour. Instead of blackberries you could use other berry fruits like strawberries or blueberries, or a mixture.

MAKES 6 PORTIONS
2 cooking apples, peeled, cored and chopped
100 g/4 oz blackberries
50 g/2 oz soft brown sugar

Cook the apples and blackberries in a saucepan with the sugar and 2 tablespoons water. Cook until the apples are soft (15–20 minutes). Put the fruit through a mouli to make into a smooth purée.

Strawberry Rice Pudding ☺ ☹

Pudding rice has a soft consistency, which is good for introducing some texture into your baby's diet. It is great mixed with fruit purée like stewed apples and pears, or add some chopped dried fruit like apricots when you are cooking the rice. You could also stir in a little strawberry jam or golden syrup.

MAKES 5 PORTIONS
50 g/2 oz pudding rice
600 ml/1 pint milk
1–2 tablespoons caster sugar
½ teaspoon vanilla essence

Put the rice, milk and sugar in a heavy-based saucepan. Bring to the boil, then reduce the heat, cover with a lid and simmer for 30–35 minutes, stirring occasionally. Mix in your favourite flavouring to serve. You can also make rice pudding in the oven. Put all the ingredients into a suitable greased dish, dot the top with butter and bake in an oven preheated to 150°C/300°F/Gas 2 for about 2 hours, stirring occasionally.

Fresh Fruit Ice Lollies

Your baby will be teething at this age and very often sore gums can put her off eating for a while. Sucking on something cold soothes sore gums so a good idea is to make fresh fruit ice lollies using puréed fruit, which you can mix with fruit juice or yoghurt. You can even pour fruit smoothies or fresh juices straight into lolly moulds. I have brought out a range of ice lolly moulds perfect for little ones (see page 208).

Raspberry and Watermelon Lollies ❄ ☺ ☹

MAKES 8 LOLLIES
¼ watermelon
60 g raspberries
40–50 g/1½–2 oz icing sugar

Cut the flesh from the watermelon and remove the seeds. Blend the watermelon and raspberries together. Strain through a sieve and stir in the icing sugar to taste. Pour into lolly moulds and freeze.

Tropical Lollies ❄ ☺ ☹

MAKES 8 LOLLIES
1 large mango, peel and stone removed, diced (approx. 350 g/12 oz flesh)
180 ml/6½ fl oz tropical fruit juice
3 tablespoons icing sugar
1 tablespoon lemon juice

Blend the ingredients together until smooth. Pour into ice lolly moulds and freeze.

Fresh Fruit with Yoghurt Dip ☺ ☹

As hand-to-eye coordination improves finger foods become a more important part of your child's diet. Start with soft fruits like banana, peach, pear or strawberries. You can also try dried fruits like apricots or apple. Your child will have fun picking up the pieces of fruit and dipping them into this tasty yoghurt.

MAKES 1 PORTION
a selection of fruit cut into pieces large enough
   for your baby to hold easily
3 tablespoons Greek yoghurt
1 teaspoon milk
1 teaspoon icing sugar
1 tablespoon lemon curd

Mix the yoghurt, milk, icing sugar and lemon curd together to make the dip.

Dried Apricots with Papaya and Pear ❄ ☺ ☹

Dried apricots are rich in betacarotene and iron and they combine well with a variety of fresh fruits. This is also good mixed with yoghurt. I found that my children also liked chewing on semi-dried apple rings which are easy to hold because of the hole in the middle.

MAKES 4 PORTIONS
50 g/2 oz ready-to-eat dried apricots
½ ripe papaya, peeled, deseeded and chopped
1 ripe juicy pear, peeled, cored and chopped

Put the apricots into a small saucepan and just cover with water. Bring to the boil and simmer until softened (about 8 minutes). Chop the apricots and mix with the chopped papaya and pear, or purée for babies who prefer a smoother texture.

Vegetables

Risotto with Butternut Squash ❄ ☺ ☹

Cooked rice with vegetables is nice and soft so it's a good way to introduce texture to your baby's food. Butternut squash is now more readily available in supermarkets and it is rich in Vitamin A. You could use pumpkin to make this, instead of squash.

MAKES 4 PORTIONS

50 g/2 oz onion, chopped
25 g/1 oz butter
100 g/4 oz basmati rice
450 ml/16 fl oz boiling water
150 g/5 oz butternut squash, peeled and chopped
3 ripe tomatoes (about 225 g/8 oz), skinned, deseeded and chopped
50 g/2 oz Cheddar cheese, grated

Sauté the onion in half the butter until softened. Stir in the rice until well coated. Pour over the boiling water, cover and cook for 8 minutes over a high heat. Stir in the butternut squash, reduce the heat and cook, covered, for about 12 minutes or until the water has been absorbed.

Meanwhile, melt the remaining butter in a small saucepan, add the chopped tomatoes and sauté for 2–3 minutes. Stir in the cheese until melted. Add the tomato and cheese mixture to the cooked rice and combine. Season to taste for babies over one year.

Lentil and Vegetable Purée ❄ ☺ ☹

Lentils are a good, cheap source of protein. They also provide iron which is very important for brain development, particularly between the ages of six months and two years. Passata is simply sieved tomatoes – you can buy it in bottles in the supermarket.

A vegetarian baby's first tastes of food is the same as for other babies (baby rice, fruit and vegetable purées etc.). But, from around seven months when proteins are being introduced, instead of meat give foods like lentils, eggs or dairy products.

It is not as easy to absorb iron from non-animal sources, so it's a good idea to give vitamin C-rich fruit or fruit juices as this helps to boost iron absorption.

MAKES 6 PORTIONS
1 tablespoon vegetable oil
50 g (2 oz) chopped onion or leek
100 g (4 oz) carrots, peeled and chopped
15g (½ oz) celery, chopped
50 g (2 oz) split red lentils
250 g (8 oz) sweet potato, peeled and chopped
200 ml (7 fl oz) passata
50 g (2 oz) mature Cheddar cheese, grated

Heat the vegetable oil and sauté the onion, carrots and celery for 5 minutes. Rinse the lentils and add to the pan. Add the sweet potato and sauté for 1 minute. Pour in the passata and 1 tablespoon of water. Cover and cook for about 30 minutes. Remove from the heat and stir in the cheese until melted. Purée in a blender.

Multicoloured Casserole ❄ ☺ ☹

Babies love the bright colours and miniature size of these vegetables. It makes eating fun, and is a good lesson in finger control.

MAKES 4 PORTIONS
1 tablespoon olive oil
1 shallot, peeled and finely chopped
40 g/1½ oz red pepper, diced
100 g/4 oz frozen peas
100 g/4 oz frozen sweetcorn
120 ml/4 fl oz vegetable stock (see page 38) or water

Heat the oil in a saucepan, add the shallot and red pepper and cook for 3 minutes. Add the peas and sweetcorn, pour over the vegetable stock and bring to the boil. Cover and simmer for 3–4 minutes.

Tasty Brown Rice ❄ ☺ ☹

Rice dishes are good for introducing more texture into your baby's food. You could also make this with white rice.

MAKES 6 PORTIONS
50 g/2 oz brown rice
1 tablespoon vegetable oil
75 g/3 oz carrots, peeled and grated
75 g/3 oz tomatoes, skinned, deseeded and chopped
40 g/1½ oz Cheddar cheese, grated

Cook the rice in water according to the packet instructions until quite soft (about 30 minutes). Meanwhile, heat the oil in a pan, add the carrots and sauté for 3 minutes. Add the tomatoes and cook for 2 more minutes. Drain the rice and mix with the carrot and tomatoes. Stir in the grated cheese and cook over a gentle heat for 1 minute until melted.

Vegetables in Cheese Sauce ✳ ☺ ☹

MAKES 6 PORTIONS
100 g/4 oz cauliflower, broken into florets
1 carrot, peeled and thinly sliced
50 g/2 oz frozen peas
100 g/4 oz courgettes, sliced

CHEESE SAUCE
25 g/1 oz margarine
2 tablespoons plain flour
250 ml/8 fl oz milk
50 g/2 oz Cheddar cheese, grated

Steam the cauliflower and carrot for 6 minutes, then add the peas and courgettes and cook for a further 4 minutes. For a young baby, cook the vegetables until they are soft.

Meanwhile make the cheese sauce in the usual way (see page 67). Mash, chop or purée the vegetables with the sauce.

Sweet Potato and Spinach Mash ☺ ☹

MAKES 3–4 PORTIONS
1 large sweet potato (approx. 375 g/13 oz)
1 large potato (approx. 200 g/7 oz)
1 medium carrot (approx. 75 g/3 oz)
60 g/2½ oz spinach leaves, washed
a generous knob of butter
1 tablespoon milk
40 g/1½ oz Cheddar cheese, grated

Peel and chop the sweet potato, potato and carrot. Put them in a saucepan and just cover with boiling water. Cook until the vegetables are tender (around 15 minutes). Alternatively you can steam the vegetables. Drain the vegetables, add the spinach to the pan and cook for 2 minutes. Mash the vegetables together with the butter, milk and cheese.

Fish

Fingers of Sole ☺☹

These fingers of sole are fun for babies and toddlers to eat, and make great finger food. They can be served plain or you can dip them into a home-made tomato sauce. Simply purée 3 skinned and deseeded tomatoes with a sautéed shallot, 1 tablespoon tomato purée, 1 dessertspoon of milk and a teaspoon of finely chopped fresh basil.

These 'fish fingers' are much better for your child than commercial ones, which are full of colouring and additives. If you are not using all the fingers at once, it is best to freeze them before they are cooked. You can then take out as many fingers as you need for a freshly cooked meal.

Crushed cornflakes also make a delicious coating for other types of fish like haddock or cod.

MAKES 8 PORTIONS
1 shallot, peeled and finely chopped
1 dessertspoon lemon juice
1 tablespoon vegetable oil
1 sole, filleted and skinned
1 egg
1 dessertspoon milk
plain flour
crushed cornflakes
a little butter or margarine for frying

Mix together the chopped shallot, lemon juice and oil. Marinate the fish fillets in this mixture for 1 hour. (If you're short of time you could skip this stage.) Remove the fillets from the marinade. Cut them into four or five diagonal strips, depending on the size of the sole. Beat the egg together with the milk. Dip the strips first into the flour, then the egg and milk and finally the crushed cornflakes. Fry the fingers in butter or margarine until golden brown on both sides. They should take no more than a few minutes to cook.

Salmon and Broccoli Pasta ❄ ☺ ☹

This recipe was sent to me by Kate Hanke, who lives in Oxford. She entered a competition that I ran together with Tumbletots, 'Eat Fit, Keep Fit', to devise a recipe that would tempt fussy eaters. Kate's tip is to stay positive, try not to show concern about your child's eating habits, or describe your child as a 'fussy eater' in front of him. If they believe they are good at eating a wide variety of healthy foods, they may well become good anyway. I found this recipe was quick, easy and very tasty. N.B. Unlike tinned tuna, tinned salmon does contain essential fatty acids.

MAKES 5 PORTIONS
250 g/12 oz animal pasta shapes
50 g/2 oz onion, finely chopped
1 garlic clove, crushed
a little butter or oil
225 g/8 oz broccoli, cut into small florets
100 g/4 oz wild tinned red salmon, drained and mashed
142 ml/5 fl oz carton single cream
50 g/2 oz Parmesan cheese, finely grated
a little freshly ground black pepper

Cook the pasta according to the packet instructions. In a large pan, fry the onion and garlic in the butter or oil until soft (about 3–4 minutes). Steam the broccoli until tender (about 6 minutes). Add the cooked pasta to the onion. Add the salmon, cream and broccoli and season with a little black pepper. Add the Parmesan cheese and mix well so that the cheese melts into the cream. Serve immediately.

Fillets of Sole with Grapes ❄ ☺ ☹

Fillets of sole with grapes makes a delicious combination. This recipe is quick and easy to prepare and one that the whole family can enjoy.

MAKES 4 ADULT PORTIONS
8 single sole fillets
1 tablespoon seasoned flour
20 g/³⁄₄ oz butter
75 g/3 oz button mushrooms, thinly sliced
100 ml/3¹⁄₂ fl oz fish stock
100 ml/3¹⁄₂ fl oz double cream
1 teaspoon lemon juice
2 teaspoons fresh parsley, chopped
20 seedless white grapes, halved
salt and pepper (from one year)

Coat the fish with seasoned flour, melt half the butter in a large frying pan and fry the fish over a medium heat for about 2 minutes on each side until lightly golden. Transfer to a plate and keep warm.

Add the remaining butter to the pan and cook the mushrooms for 3 minutes. Add the stock and simmer for 2 minutes. Stir in the cream and lemon juice and then simmer for 2 minutes. Add the parsley and grapes, then season with salt and pepper (if using) and pour over the fish.

Salmon with a Creamy Chive Sauce ❄ ☺ ☹

Salmon is easy to cook. It can be cooked very quickly in the microwave but here I have wrapped it in aluminium foil with some vegetables and herbs and cooked it more slowly to bring out the flavour.

MAKES 5 PORTIONS

200 g/8 oz fillet of salmon or 1 small salmon cutlet
1 dessertspoon lemon juice
½ small onion, peeled and sliced
½ bay leaf
1 small tomato, cut into chunks
1 sprig of fresh parsley
a little butter

CHIVE SAUCE

15 g/½ oz butter
1 tablespoon plain flour
150 ml/5 fl oz milk
cooking liquid from the fish
1 dessertspoon fresh chives, snipped

Wrap the salmon in aluminium foil with the rest of the ingredients and bake in an oven preheated to 180°C/350°F/Gas 4 for 15 minutes. Meanwhile, make a white sauce, using the butter, flour and milk in the usual way (see page 67).

Once the salmon is cooked, remove it from the foil, strain off the cooking liquid and add this to the white sauce. Finally, stir the chives into the sauce. Flake the salmon and pour the chive sauce over it.

Salmon Footballs ❄ ☺ ☹

When your child refuses to eat anything from a spoon, these make nutritious finger foods. Omit the salt and pepper for babies under one year.

MAKES 10 SMALL FOOTBALLS

1 medium potato, skin on (approx. 150 g/5 oz)
70 g/2¾ oz salmon fillet
a squeeze of lemon juice
a knob of butter
2 spring onions, chopped
1 teaspoon sweet chilli sauce (optional)
2 tablespoons tomato ketchup
½ tablespoon mayonnaise
1 tablespoon seasoned flour
1 egg, lightly beaten
50 g/2 oz breadcrumbs
sunflower oil for frying
salt and freshly ground black pepper (from one year)

Boil the potato in salted water for 25–30 minutes until tender when pierced with a table knife. Drain and when cool enough to handle, peel and mash.

Cook the salmon in the microwave on High for 2–3 minutes with a squeeze of lemon juice and a knob of butter. Flake the flesh onto a plate and leave to cool slightly. Mix the potato with the spring onions, chilli sauce (if using), tomato ketchup, mayonnaise, and salt and pepper to taste. Fold in the flaked salmon, being careful not to break up the fish too much.

Take 1½ tablespoons of the mixture and form into a ball. Repeat until you have used up all the mixture. Dust each ball in the seasoned flour, dip in the egg and then roll in the breadcrumbs.

Heat some sunflower oil in a non-stick pan and deep-fry the footballs for 2–3 minutes. You can shallow fry the footballs in 2 tablespoons of oil but they won't keep their round shape so well.

Chicken

Chicken and Apple Balls ❄ ☺ ☹

This is a great favourite with my family. Grated apple adds a delicious flavour to these chicken balls, which makes them appealing to young children, and they are delicious hot or cold. These little balls make perfect finger food.

MAKES 20 CHICKEN BALLS
2 teaspoons light olive oil
1 onion, finely chopped
1 large Granny Smith apple, peeled and grated
2 large chicken breasts, cut into chunks
½ tablespoon fresh parsley, chopped
1 tablespoon fresh thyme or sage, chopped, or a pinch mixed dried herbs
1 chicken stock cube, crumbled (from one year)
50 g/2 oz fresh white breadcrumbs
salt and freshly ground pepper (from one year)
plain flour for coating
vegetable oil for frying

Heat the olive oil in a pan and sauté half the onion for about 3 minutes. Using your hands, squeeze out a little excess liquid from the grated apple. Mix the apple with the chicken, cooked and remaining raw onion, herbs, stock cube (from one year) and breadcrumbs and roughly chop in a food processor for a few seconds. Season with a little salt and pepper (from one year).

With your hands, form into about 20 little balls, roll in flour and fry in shallow oil for about 5 minutes until lightly golden and cooked through.

Bang Bang Chicken ❄ ☺ ☹

So called because my son liked to help flatten the chicken by banging it with a mallet! If you want to prepare these chicken fingers in advance wrap each strip separately (before frying) and freeze. Just take one or two strips out of the freezer and fry them for freshly cooked chicken fingers.

MAKES 8 PORTIONS
2 chicken breasts, off the bone and skinned
3 slices bread, crusts removed
1½ tablespoons grated Parmesan cheese (optional)
1 tablespoon fresh parsley, chopped (optional)
plain flour for coating
1 egg, beaten
vegetable oil

Cover the chicken with greaseproof paper and flatten with a mallet or rolling pin, then cut each breast lengthways into four strips. Make breadcrumbs from the slices of bread in a food processor. If you are using the Parmesan and parsley, mix these together with the breadcrumbs in a bowl.

Dip the chicken into the flour, then into the egg and then finally into the breadcrumbs. Fry in oil for 3–4 minutes each side until golden on the outside and cooked through. Drain on absorbent kitchen paper and serve.

Chicken with Cornflakes ❄ ☺ ☹

Cornflakes are very versatile and I often use them instead of breadcrumbs to coat both chicken and fish. These strips of chicken make good finger food. Before cooking, they can be individually wrapped and frozen.

MAKES 3–4 PORTIONS
1 egg, beaten
1 tablespoon milk
25 g/1 oz cornflakes, crushed
1 large chicken breast, skinned, off the bone and cut into about 8 strips
15 g/½ oz butter, melted

Mix together the egg and milk in a shallow dish. In a separate dish spread out the cornflake crumbs. Dip the strips of chicken first into the egg and then coat with the cornflakes. Put the chicken strips into a greased ovenproof dish, drizzle over the melted butter and toss to coat. Bake in an oven preheated to 180°C/350°F/Gas 4 for about 10 minutes on each side or until cooked through. Alternatively, the chicken strips can be sautéed in vegetable oil until golden and cooked through.

Chicken with Summer Vegetables ❄ ☺ ☹

The sweet potato, apple juice and peas add a natural sweetness that babies like. The garlic and basil adds flavour, which is important since you can't add salt before one year of age.

MAKES 5 PORTIONS

1 small onion, chopped
½ small sweet red pepper, deseeded and finely chopped
1½ tablespoons olive oil
1 garlic clove, crushed
1 chicken breast (approx. 125 g/4½ oz), cut into pieces
2 tablespoons apple juice
175 ml/6 fl oz chicken stock (see page 76)
1 medium courgette, chopped (approx. 100 g/4 oz)
200 g/7 oz sweet potato, peeled and chopped
50 g/2 oz frozen peas
1 tablespoon fresh basil, torn

Sauté the onion and sweet pepper in the olive oil until softened. Add the garlic and sauté for 1 minute. Stir in the chicken and continue to cook for 3–4 minutes. Pour over the apple juice and stock and stir in the courgette and sweet potato. Bring to the boil, then cover and simmer for about 8 minutes. Stir in the peas and continue to cook for 3 minutes. Chop or pureé to the desired consistency.

Chicken with Winter Vegetables ❄ ☺ ☹

This is quick and easy to prepare and has a delicious rich chicken flavour.

MAKES 6 PORTIONS
1 chicken breast, on the bone and skinned
a little flour
vegetable oil
1 leek, white part only, washed and sliced
1 small onion, peeled and finely chopped
3 carrots, peeled and sliced
1 celery stalk, trimmed and sliced
400 ml/14 fl oz chicken stock (see page 76)

Cut the chicken breast in half, roll each half in flour and brown in a little oil for 3–4 minutes. In another frying pan, sauté the leek and onion in a little oil for 5 minutes until soft and golden. Put the chicken into a casserole together with all the vegetables and the stock. Cook in an oven preheated to 180°C/350°F/Gas 4 for 1 hour, stirring halfway through.

Take the chicken off the bone and chop it into little pieces with the vegetables or purée it together with the cooking liquid in a mouli or blender.

Chicken with Couscous ❄ ☺ ☹

MAKES 4 PORTIONS
15 g/½ oz butter
25 g/1 oz chopped onion
25 g/1 oz frozen peas (cooked)
175 ml/6 fl oz chicken stock (see page 76)
65 g/2½ oz quick-cooking couscous
50 g/2 oz diced cooked chicken

Melt the butter in a saucepan and sauté the onion until softened but not coloured. Stir in the peas, pour over the stock, bring to the boil and cook for 3 minutes. Stir in the couscous, remove from the heat, cover and set aside for 6 minutes. Fluff the couscous with a fork and mix in the diced chicken.

Red meats

Beef Casserole with Carrots ✻ ☺ ☹

The secret for a delicious rich taste is to cook the meat for a long time so that it is very tender and has a good flavour from the onions and carrots. Increase the Marmite for toddlers.

MAKES 10 PORTIONS
2 medium onions, peeled and sliced
vegetable oil
350 g/12 oz lean stewing beef, trimmed and cut into small chunks
2 medium carrots, peeled and sliced
1 beef stock cube, crumbled or 1 teaspoon Marmite (for babies over one year)
1 tablespoon fresh parsley, chopped
600 ml/1 pint water
2 large potatoes, cut into quarters

Fry the onion until golden in a little oil, then add the meat chunks and brown. Transfer the meat and onions to a small casserole and add all the rest of the ingredients except for the potatoes. Cook, covered, in an oven preheated to 180°C/350°F/Gas 4 for 30 minutes, then turn down the heat and cook for a further 2½ hours at 160°C/325°F/Gas 3. An hour before you finish cooking the meat, add the potatoes.

Chop the casserole quite finely in a food processor or blender so that it is easy for your baby to chew. If the meat gets too dry whilst cooking, add a little extra water. You can also add mushrooms and tomatoes to this recipe for variation and they should be added 30 minutes before the end of cooking time.

Tasty Liver Casserole ❄ ☺ ☺

Liver is very good for children: it is easy to digest, a good source of iron and is very easy to cook. I must admit that I dislike the taste having been forced to eat liver at school, but, to my great surprise, my one-year-old son adored it. This recipe is good served with mashed potato.

MAKES 4 PORTIONS
100 g/4 oz calf's liver, trimmed and sliced
2 tablespoons vegetable oil
1 small onion, peeled and chopped
1 large or 2 medium carrots (approx. 125 g/4½ oz), peeled and chopped
200 ml/7 fl oz chicken or vegetable stock (see pages 76 and 38)
2 medium tomatoes (approx. 200 g/7 oz), skinned, deseeded and chopped
1 dessertspoon fresh parsley, chopped

Sauté the liver in 1 tablespoon of the oil until browned, then set aside. Heat the remaining oil in a saucepan and sauté the onion for 2–3 minutes. Add the chopped carrot and sauté for 2 minutes, then pour over the stock, bring to the boil, cover and simmer over a low heat for about 15 minutes. Chop the liver into pieces and add to the pan together with the tomatoes and parsley, and cook for about 3 minutes. You can either serve with mashed potato as it is or blend the mixture for a few seconds to make a rough purée.

Savoury Veal Casserole ❄ ☺ ☺

A delicious casserole of veal, vegetables and fresh herbs – just increase the quantities for a meal the whole family can enjoy.

MAKES 3 PORTIONS
1 small onion, peeled and finely chopped
1 carrot, scraped and sliced
½ celery stalk, sliced
vegetable oil
100 g/4 oz lean veal for stewing

1 sprig of fresh rosemary
1 sprig of fresh parsley
120 ml/4 fl oz water

Fry the onion, carrot and celery in a little oil for 3 minutes. Cut the veal into chunks and put it into a saucepan with the vegetables, herbs and the water. Simmer slowly, covered for 1 hour (stirring once). Remove the herbs and roughly chop the veal and vegetables in a food processor.

Special Steak ✳ ☺ ☺

This recipe makes a very good introduction to red meat for your baby.

MAKES 4 PORTIONS
1 potato (about 225 g/8 oz), peeled and chopped
1 shallot or 25 g/1 oz onion, peeled and finely chopped
1 tablespoon vegetable oil
100 g/4 oz fillet steak
50 g/2 oz button mushrooms, washed and chopped
15 g/½ oz butter
1 tomato, skinned, deseeded and chopped
2 tablespoons milk

Boil the potato until tender, then drain. Meanwhile, sauté the shallot in the vegetable oil until softened. Spoon half the shallots on to a piece of aluminium foil. Cut the steak into slices 1 cm/½ inch thick and place on top of the shallots. Spread the remaining shallots over the steak. Cook under a preheated grill for 3 minutes each side or until cooked. Sauté the button mushrooms in half of the butter for 2 minutes, add the chopped tomato and continue to cook for 1 minute. Mash the potato with the milk and the remaining butter until smooth. Chop or purée the steak together with the shallots, mushrooms and tomato and mix with the mashed potato.

Mini Cottage Pie ❄ ☺ ☹

Cottage pie was always popular as 'comfort food' on a winter's evening when I was a child. To make it suitable for babies I have chopped the meat in a food processor to make it softer. For babies over one you can season with a little salt and pepper. Try making individual portions in ramekin dishes. You can pop the extra portions in the freezer for days when you don't have time to cook.

MAKES 3 PORTIONS

100 g/4 oz carrot, peeled and chopped
225 g/8 oz potatoes, peeled and chopped
1 tablespoon olive oil
1 small onion, peeled and chopped
25 g/1 oz red pepper cored, deseeded and diced
1 small garlic clove, peeled and crushed
175 g/6 oz lean minced beef
1 tablespoon freshly chopped parsley
2 teaspoons tomato purée
100 ml/3½ fl oz chicken stock (see page 76)
15 g/½ oz butter
1 tablespoon milk
1 egg, beaten

Put the carrot into a saucepan, cover with boiling water and cook for 5 minutes. Add the potatoes and cook for a further 15 minutes.

Meanwhile, heat the oil in a frying pan and sauté the onion and red pepper for 3 to 4 minutes. Add the garlic and sauté for 1 minute. Add the minced beef and sauté until browned. At this stage it is a good idea to chop the meat in a food processor for a few seconds to give it a smoother texture. Return to the pan, add the parsley, tomato purée and chicken stock, bring to the boil, then cover and simmer for about 5 minutes. When the potato and carrot are cooked, drain and mash with the butter and milk.

Spoon the meat into 3 ramekins about 10 cm/4 inches in diameter. Top with the mashed potato and carrot. Brush with a little beaten egg, then heat through in an oven preheated to 180°C/350°F/Gas 4, then place under a preheated grill until lightly golden.

Tasty Rice with Meat and Vegetables ❄ ☺ ☹

MAKES 8 PORTIONS
½ onion, peeled and finely chopped
65 g/2½ oz carrot, finely chopped
1 tablespoon vegetable oil
1 small garlic clove, crushed
225 g/8 oz lean minced beef
400 g/14 oz canned chopped tomatoes
a few drops of Worcestershire sauce

RICE
50 g/2 oz basmati rice
300 ml/10 fl oz chicken stock (see page 76)
½ small red pepper, deseeded and finely chopped
50 g/2 oz frozen peas

Rinse the rice and place in a saucepan with the chicken stock. Bring to the boil, then cover and simmer for 10 minutes. Add the red pepper and cook, uncovered, for 5 minutes. Add the peas and continue to cook for 2 minutes, or until the rice is tender and there is no liquid left.

Meanwhile sauté the onion and carrot in the vegetable oil for 5 minutes. Add the garlic and sauté for 1 minute. Add the minced meat and cook, stirring, until browned. Transfer the meat into a food processor and chop for 30 seconds to make it easier for your baby to chew. Return the meat to the pan and add the tomatoes and Worcestershire sauce. Cook over a low heat for 10 minutes. Stir in the rice with vegetables and cook for 3–4 minutes.

Pasta

Pasta Shell Confetti ❄ ☺ ☹

I used to get so many requests for tiny pasta shapes that I brought out my own range of mini-organic pasta, ranging from tiny gluten-free pasta stars to organic mini pasta shells and novelty pasta like animals and alphabet shapes. You can mix the Pasta Shell Confetti with lots of different vegetables – peas and broccoli would make a good combination.

MAKES 2–3 PORTIONS
15 g/½ oz butter
40 g/1½ oz carrot, peeled and diced
40 g/1½ oz courgette, topped, tailed and diced
1 medium tomato, skinned, deseeded and chopped (approx. 40 g/1½ oz)
60 g tiny pasta shapes (e.g. mini organic pasta shells, see page 208)
3 tablespoons single cream
30 g/1¼ oz grated Parmesan cheese

Melt the butter and sauté the carrot for 3 minutes. Add the courgette and cook gently for 8 minutes. Add the tomato and cook for 1 more minute.

Cook the pasta in plenty of boiling water for 6 minutes. Drain the pasta and stir into the vegetables. Remove from the heat and stir in the cream and Parmesan cheese.

Bolognese Sauce with Aubergine ❄ ☺ ☹

MAKES 12 PORTIONS OF SAUCE

1 medium onion, peeled and chopped
¼ garlic clove, peeled and chopped
vegetable oil for frying
450 g/1 lb lean minced beef or lamb
2 tablespoons tomato purée
4 tomatoes, skinned, deseeded and chopped
¼ teaspoon mixed dried herbs
2 tablespoons plain flour
450 ml/16 fl oz chicken stock (see page 76)
1 aubergine, peeled and sliced
100 g/4 oz mushrooms, washed and sliced

Sauté the onion and garlic in oil until soft. Add the meat and cook until browned.
Chop in a food processor. Return to the pan, add the tomato purée, tomatoes,
herbs, flour and stock. Bring to the boil and simmer for 45 minutes. Fry the
aubergine in oil until golden. Pat dry with kitchen paper. Chop in a food processor.
Sauté the mushrooms in oil and add to the sauce with the aubergine.

Pasta Shells with Hidden Vegetable Bolognese ❄ ☺ ☹

A tasty tomato-based sauce with five vegetables blended in.

MAKES 8 PORTIONS

2 tablespoons olive oil
1 small red onion, finely chopped
1 small leek, finely sliced
3 mushrooms, sliced
1 carrot, grated
1 stick celery, diced
1 garlic clove, crushed
150 ml/5 fl oz beef or chicken stock (see page 76)
250 g/9 oz minced beef
2 x 400 g cans chopped tomatoes
3 tablespoons tomato purée
1 tablespoon sun-dried tomato paste
1 x 250 g packet mini pasta shells

Heat 1 tablespoon of the olive oil in a pan and sauté the onion for 3 minutes. Add the leek, mushrooms, carrot and celery and sauté for 7 minutes. Add the garlic and sauté for 1 minute. Add half of the stock and simmer for 10 minutes, then put in a food processor and blitz. Heat the remaining tablespoon of olive oil in a large frying pan and brown the minced beef for 5 minutes, breaking up well with a fork or wooden spoon. Add the chopped tomatoes, tomato puree, sun-dried tomato paste and the remaining stock, and cook for 10 minutes. Add the blended vegetables and continue to cook for 2 minutes.

Meanwhile, cook the pasta according to the packet instructions. Drain and toss with the sauce.

Pasta Shells with Chicken and Broccoli ❄ ☺ ☹

MAKES 2 PORTIONS

40 g/1½ oz broccoli florets
15 g/½ oz butter
15 g/½ oz flour
150 ml/5 fl oz milk
30 g/1¼ oz Gruyère cheese, grated
3 tablespoons Parmesan cheese, grated
3 tablespoons mascarpone cheese
40 g/1½ oz pasta shells
30 g/1¼ oz cooked chicken, diced

Steam the broccoli for 4–5 minutes or until tender. Melt the butter, stir in the flour and cook for 1 minute. Gradually add the milk, then continue to stir for 5 minutes over a low heat until the sauce thickens. Take off the heat, stir in the Gruyère and Parmesan until melted, then stir in the mascarpone.

Meanwhile, cook the pasta according to the packet instructions. Drain and toss with the broccoli, chicken and cheese sauce.

Pasta Stars with Veggie Sauce ❄ ☺ ☹

This fresh tomato sauce is very tasty and, because it has vegetables and cheese blended into it, it is more nutritious than an ordinary tomato sauce.

MAKES 2 PORTIONS
1 medium carrot, peeled and sliced
100 g/4 oz cauliflower florets
3 tablespoons pasta stars or other tiny pasta shapes
25 g/1 oz butter
300 g/11 oz ripe tomatoes, skinned, deseeded and chopped
50 g/2 oz grated Cheddar cheese

Put the sliced carrot into the bottom of a steamer. Cover with boiling water and cook over a medium heat for 10 minutes. Put the cauliflower florets in the steamer basket, place over the carrots, cover and cook for 5 minutes or until the vegetables are tender. Cook the pasta stars in boiling water according to the packet instructions. Meanwhile, melt the butter and sauté the tomatoes for about 3 minutes or until mushy. Stir in the Cheddar cheese until melted. Blend the cooked carrots and cauliflower together with the tomatoes and cheese. Mix with the pasta stars.

Nine to twelve month meal planner

	Breakfast	Mid-morning	Lunch	Mid-afternoon	Dinner	Bedtime
Day 1	Fruity Swiss Muesli Dried Apricots with Papaya and Pear served with yoghurt Milk	Milk	Chicken and Apple Balls Finger vegetables Strawberry Rice Pudding Water	Milk	Finger sandwiches Finger vegetables Juice or water	Milk
Day 2	Weetabix Cheese on toast Fruit Milk	Milk	Special Steak Fresh fruit and yoghurt dip Water	Milk	**Pasta Stars with Veggie Sauce** Fromage frais/Yoghurt Juice or water	Milk
Day 3	Scrambled egg with toast Fruit with cottage cheese Milk	Milk	**Salmon Footballs Fresh Fruit Ice Lollies** Water	Milk	**Tasty Brown Rice** Fruit Juice or water	Milk
Day 4	**My Favourite Pancakes** Fruit Milk	Milk	**Mini Cottage Pie** Fruit Water	Milk	**Vegetables in Cheese Sauce Apple and Blackberry** Juice or water	Milk

	Breakfast	Mid-morning	Lunch	Mid-afternoon	Dinner	Bedtime
Day 5	French Toast Cut-Outs Apricot, Apple and Pear Custard Milk	Milk	Bang Bang Chicken Tasty Brown Rice Fresh fruit with yoghurt dip Water	Milk	Risotto and Butternut Squash Fruit Juice or water	Milk
Day 6	**Summer Fruit Muesli** Yoghurt with dried fruit Milk	Milk	**Pasta Shells with Hidden Vegetable Bolognese Apple and Blackberry** Water	Milk	**Fingers of Sole** Finger vegetables **Fresh Fruit Ice Lollies** Juice or water	Milk
Day 7	Cheese Scramble Toast Fingers Yoghurt Milk	Milk	Chicken with Couscous Fresh fruit with yoghurt dip Water	Milk	Lentil and Vegetable Purée Sticks of cheese **Baked Apples with Raisins** Juice or water	Milk

I find that, beyond the age of one, toddlers prefer to exercise their independence and feed themselves. The more your toddler experiments using a spoon and fork, the quicker he will master the art of feeding himself – you never know, some food might find its way into his mouth! A 'pelican' bib – a strong plastic bib which has a tray at the bottom to catch stray food – is also good. If your toddler has difficulty eating with a spoon, try giving him finger foods like goujons of fish or raw vegetables with a dip. You must still be careful, though, to keep food like olives, nuts or fresh lychees out of the reach of young children. Toddlers love to put everything in their mouths and it would be so easy for them to choke on such foods.

Enjoying mealtimes together

Toddlers only have small tummies and often can't eat enough at mealtimes to fuel their high energy requirements, so they should be offered three meals and snacks at regular times. It's a good idea to have a shelf in your fridge with some healthy snacks like raw vegetables and a dip e.g. hummus, sticks of cheese and a variety of fresh fruit. For more ideas for healthy snacks, take a look at my book After-School Meal Planner. Toddlers who get used to eating healthy snacks are more likely to continue the same habits later on in life. However, it would also be wrong to make sweets and chocolate biscuits the forbidden fruit, as your toddler would crave them all the more and gorge himself on them whenever he could.

Many toddlers enjoy eating much more sophisticated food than we would imagine. My daughter at two loved olives, for example. Ethnic recipes like stir fries with noodles or egg-fried rice with chicken tend to be popular and you can buy child-friendly chopsticks that are joined at the top and make eating fun. Dump the chicken dinosaurs covered in breadcrumbs and marinate chicken to make recipes like my Thai-style Chicken and Noodles or Chicken Satay (see pages 170 and 172). Even if you don't feel like making your own marinade, there are lots of delicious marinades in the supermarket that will spice up your child's food. Let your child try food from your plate and you may be very surprised by the tastes he enjoys. Of course, food from Mummy's or Daddy's plate is much more interesting than his own meal and you can sometimes entice your child to eat if you put his meal on your plate. But the point at this stage is that the toddler can now eat, to a large extent, what you adults are eating. I am a great believer in giving toddlers 'grown-up' foods as soon as possible and almost all the recipes that follow are suitable for the whole family. Do eat with your child rather than just sitting there shovelling food into his mouth. He'll eat much more happily with you – after all, who enjoys eating alone?

Try and reform your own eating habits by adding less salt and sugar to your food and get your child to help plan, shop for and cook a meal. Obviously you can't do this every day but if you do it every so often, it's a good way of introducing new meals to your child.

My Child Won't Eat!

Anyone with a fussy child will know that it's easy to lose heart when your child turns his nose up at anything with visible onions or tomato sauce with green bits in it. I think the key to success is not to get into a tizz if your child doesn't eat – just say 'fine', but don't offer anything else until the next meal. Refusing food loses its appeal if you don't react and it's amazing how much less fussy your child will become if he is really hungry. I would ignore any negative behaviour and pile on the praise when your child does try something – even if the tiniest morsel passes his lips, go overboard with praise. A star chart might be a good idea, where your child gets a star for any new food or recipe that he tries. When he collects a certain number of stars he gets a reward.

Rest assured that if you have a fussy toddler you are not alone. Toddlers can thrive very well on remarkably little food. They are also unpredictable – one day they can like something and the next day they refuse to eat it. Some days they will be ravenous and other days they will eat practically nothing. If you monitor your child's food intake over a whole week, you won't worry as much if one day he refuses to eat anything.

Often it's snacks between meals that spoil your child's appetite. Try to resist buying chocolate biscuits and crisps and instead offer healthy alternatives like mini-sandwiches, dried fruit or even a bowl of healthy cereal.

Check your child isn't filling up on drinks. What he drinks can have a huge effect on his appetite. Give juice or smoothies that are 100 per cent juice instead of fruit juice drinks, which often contain less than 10 per cent juice and can contain artificial sweeteners, flavourings and colourings, as well as added sugar – some with more than six teaspoons of sugar in a glass. Tap water is the best way to quench your thirst, and it's safe, cheap and calorie-free.

A gift wrapped in bright paper with a beautiful ribbon inspires more enthusiasm than one given in a brown cardboard box, and the same goes for food that we serve our kids. You can transform a plain-Jane peanut butter sandwich into an irresistible kids' treat when it's cut into a heart or a teddy bear shape. Instead of whole fruit in a fruit bowl, thread bite-sized pieces of fruit onto a skewer or straw, or purée fruit and freeze it in ice lolly moulds.

Don't put too much food on a plate – much better that your child should ask for more. Toddlers love individual portions of food and it's good to make mini portions of larger pies.

Getting children to try something new is not easy – of my three children two were quite fussy so I've tried all the tricks myself. Inviting a child over for tea who is a good eater is an excellent ruse. At all costs avoid confrontation – it's much better to turn 'weird' food into a game by blindfolding your child and then asking him to try a selection of foods, some familiar and some new, and then guess what they are …

If you enjoy the recipes in this chapter look out for my sequel to this book, *Favourite Family Recipes*.

The Foods to Choose

Children under five need more dietary fat than adults in proportion to their body weight so unless your child is overweight, don't give him foods that are low-fat. Fats like cheese or full fat yoghurt are a rich source of energy which your toddler needs to fuel his growth. There are, of course, exceptions to the rule, and an overweight toddler should have his fat intake restricted by cutting down on processed and fatty foods and switching to low-fat dairy products.

High-fibre foods in large amounts are also unsuitable as they are bulky and filling and do not supply enough calories for a rapidly growing toddler. Also, a high-fibre diet can hinder the absorption of vital minerals like iron. Provided your child eats plenty of fruit and vegetables he will get all the fibre he needs.

Once your child is twelve months old you can switch from formula to whole cow's milk, but don't give semi-skimmed milk before the age of two as it is low in calories, which your child needs to grow. Skimmed milk should not be introduced before five years. Children over one year need 400 ml/14 fl oz of whole milk a day. For children who are very picky, there may be advantages to continuing with a follow-on formula (which is fortified with vitamins and iron) until two years of age.

Although more and more people seem to be turning away from red meat in favour of fish and chicken, bear in mind that red meat provides more iron and zinc than either fish or poultry. Try making tasty meals with lean minced meat – a good tip is to cook the meat and then chop it in a food processor so that it is not lumpy, and there are some lovely recipes for Beefburgers, Meatballs and Mini Minute steaks (see pages 178–81) that make excellent family meals. Try to avoid processed meats like sausages, salami and corned beef.

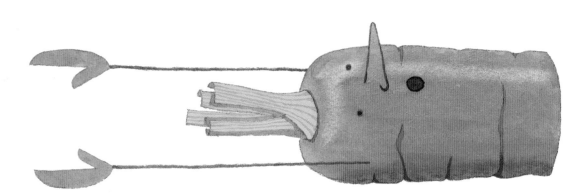

Iron deficiency and anaemia can cause difficult behaviour and poor concentration in toddlers.

If you are bringing your child up on a vegetarian diet or if he simply dislikes eating meat, make sure that you include nutrient-dense foods like cheese and eggs in his diet. Avoid giving too many high-fibre foods like wholegrain cereals and pulses as tummies fill up quickly and your child may not get enough energy and protein to grow. Provided your toddler is eating a good variety of food types, a vegetarian diet can provide all the nutrients he needs. It is very important to include vegetarian sources of iron such as green vegetables, pulses, fortified breakfast cereals and dried fruit every day, and make sure you give foods or drinks containing Vitamin C at the same meal as this helps to boost the iron absorption from non-meat sources.

Pasta remains a great favourite with toddlers and you can combine it with other healthy foods such as vegetables and tuna. Individual pieces of pasta like penne or fusilli tend to be easiest for toddlers to eat. (Although, when my son, Nicholas, was 20 months old he invented his own method of eating spaghetti – he held it out in front of him by the two ends and sucked in from the middle! Not the height of good manners perhaps, but certainly very efficient.)

Junk food substitutes

Three quarters of the salt and saturated fat that children consume comes from processed foods and ready meals. Most children eat twice as much salt as they should. It's much better to make your own healthy 'junk food' – try my delicious recipes for Annabel's Tasty Beefburgers or Home-made Fast Food Pizza (see pages 178 and 158).

Here are some substitutes for 'junk food':

Sugar-coated breakfast cereals	Porridge, Weetabix or muesli
Chicken nuggets	Chicken on the Griddle (page 174) or Bar-B-Q Chicken (page 171)
Fish fingers	Fish Pie (page 164) or Salmon Fishcakes (page 160)
Spaghetti Hoops	Pasta with Hidden-Vegetable Tomato Sauce (page 156)
Sausages	Cocktail Meatballs (page 180) or Mini Minute Steaks (page 181)
Crisps	Popcorn
Juice drinks	Pure fruit juice

Fruit and Desserts

There are many recipes in this chapter for delicious hot and cold desserts that are easy to prepare and can be enjoyed by the whole family. However, there is still nothing more delicious or better for you than fresh ripe fruit, so make sure your child has plenty of it every day. None of the vitamins or nutrients are destroyed through cooking, and fruit makes great finger food for your toddler.

Fruits are packed with powerful antioxidants and natural compounds called phytochemicals, which help boost immunity and protect the body from heart disease and cancer. The incidence of cancer is increasing. Approximately one third of cancer cases are related to what we eat and researchers estimate that a diet filled with fruit and vegetables instead of fats and processed foods, along with exercise, could reduce the incidence of cancer by at least 30 per cent.

Whole fruit in a fruit bowl isn't that appealing to a hungry child, but if you have a selection of fresh fruit cut up and placed on a low shelf in the fridge, or bite-sized fruit on a skewer, this will help stop your child from snacking on crisps or chocolate biscuits.

Dried fruits, especially apricots, are very nutritious as the drying process concentrates the nutrients. However, take care not to give dried fruit too often in between meals, as they stick to the teeth and even natural sugars cause tooth decay.

Kiwi fruit and citrus and berry fruits are rich in Vitamin C, which helps to boost iron absorption, so try to make sure you include these in your child's diet. You can add fresh or dried fruits to breakfast cereals. It's also worth buying a juicer so you can make your own fresh-fruit smoothies. Pure fruit juice and smoothies are also good, but be wary of fruit juice drinks as they often contain as little as 10 per cent juice so always read the label. Juices are a great source of vitamins but remember that only by eating the whole fruit will your child be getting fibre.

As different fruits provide different nutrients, include as much variety as possible in your child's diet. Try introducing him to some more exotic fruits. One kiwi fruit contains more than the daily adult requirement of Vitamin C and makes a good snack when cut in half, placed in an egg cup and eaten with a teaspoon. You could also make a tropical fruit salad with mango, melon balls, pineapple and a sauce made with fresh orange juice and passion fruit.

You can make delicious and healthy ice lollies from puréed fresh fruits, yoghurt, fruit juices or smoothies. Ice lolly moulds are cheap to buy, and one food that almost no child can resist is an ice lolly so this is a good way to encourage children to eat more fruit.

Ice creams in all colours, shapes and sizes are sold all over the world. However, the quality of some products is put to shame by the genuine, home-made experience. If you do buy ice creams, choose those that are made from natural ingredients only. If you want to try your hand at making your own, it really is worth investing in an ice-cream-making machine, which churns the mixture as it freezes. Believe me, you will put it to good use over the years and your children will be very popular with their friends when they come round for tea.

Quantities

In this chapter, I have given quantities in adult portions. Every child is different and you must gauge the portion size on your toddler's appetite. He can eat anything from a quarter of an adult portion to a whole portion if he is exceptionally hungry and greedy!

Food additives, particularly artificial colourings, have been blamed for causing hyperactivity in children and are linked with problems such as ADHD. To cut down on additives try to make the majority of your family's food yourself. You may well see a big change in your child's behaviour.

Overweight toddlers

In the UK, more than one in five children under the age of four is overweight, and one in ten six-year-olds is obese. If your child is overweight, then you should discuss with your doctor the best ways of decreasing his calorie intake. Adopt a healthier eating plan rather than cutting down on the amount of food offered. No child should ever go hungry. Cut out sugary, fatty and processed foods and give more fresh fruit and vegetables. Give high-fibre and wholegrain cereals like Weetabix, porridge or bran flakes. Give jacket potatoes instead of chips, griddled or grilled skewers, grilled or roast chicken instead of chicken nuggets, and fish without breadcrumbs. Semi-skimmed milk can be introduced from two years.

There are over one million obese children in the UK. Interestingly, 90 per cent of junk food is bought by parents for their children.

Special Fried Rice ☺ ☹

Babies love rice and this is very appealing as it is so colourful. For older children you can make little sailing boats. Cut a cooked red pepper in half, stuff each half with rice and stick two corn chips upright in the rice to look like sails. For non-vegetarians you could add diced chicken, ham or prawns.

MAKES 6 ADULT PORTIONS

225 g/8 oz basmati rice
75 g/3 oz carrots, scrubbed and diced
75 g/3 oz frozen peas
75 g/3 oz sweet red pepper, deseeded and diced
3 tablespoons vegetable oil or vegetable oil with
   a teaspoon of sesame oil
2 eggs, lightly beaten
1 small onion, peeled and finely chopped
1 spring onion, finely sliced
1 tablespoon soy sauce

Wash the rice thoroughly and cook according to the packet instructions in a saucepan of lightly salted water until tender. Steam the carrot, peas and pepper for 5 minutes or until tender. Heat 1 tablespoon of the oil in a frying pan. Season the eggs with a little salt, add to the pan, tilting it so the eggs form a thin layer over the bottom, and fry until set like a very thin omelette. Remove from the pan and cut into thin strips. Meanwhile, put 2 tablespoons of oil into a wok or frying pan and sauté the chopped onion until softened. Add the steamed vegetables and rice and cook, stirring, for 2–3 minutes. Add the egg and spring onion and cook, stirring, for 2 minutes more. Sprinkle with the soy sauce before serving.

Stuffed Potatoes ✲ ☺ ☹

Stuffed potatoes make an excellent meal for toddlers and there are endless variations on the fillings you can make. Prick medium potatoes all over and brush with oil. Bake in an oven preheated to 190°C/375°F/Gas 5 for 1¼–1½ hours or until tender. Alternatively, to speed up the cooking, prick the potatoes, wrap them in absorbent kitchen paper and put them in the microwave on high for 7–8 minutes. Brush the potatoes with oil and then transfer to the oven and cook for about 45–50 minutes or until tender.

Carefully spoon the soft flesh out of the skins, leaving enough round the sides for the skins to keep their shape. You are now ready to make the various fillings.

Vegetable and Cheese Potato Filling ✲ ☺ ☹

MAKES 4 ADULT PORTIONS
25 g/1 oz each broccoli and cauliflower, broken into small florets
4 medium or 2 large baked potatoes
15 g/½ oz butter
120 ml/4 fl oz milk
50 g/2 oz Cheddar cheese, grated
2 medium tomatoes, skinned and cut into small pieces
½ teaspoon salt
Cheddar cheese, grated, to finish

Steam the broccoli and cauliflower florets until they are tender (about 6 minutes), then chop finely. Meanwhile, mash the potato flesh with the butter and milk until smooth and creamy. Mix in the cheese, tomatoes, cooked chopped vegetables and salt, and scoop the mixture back into the potato skins. Sprinkle a little extra grated cheese on top and brown under a preheated grill.

Tuna and Sweetcorn Stuffed Potato ❄ ☺ ☹

If you don't have time to oven-bake the potatoes you can bake them in a microwave, although they won't have crispy skins.

MAKES 2 ADULT PORTIONS
2 medium baked potatoes
200 g/7 oz canned tuna in oil, drained
75 g/3 oz canned or cooked frozen sweetcorn
2 tablespoons mayonnaise
2 tablespoons milk
2 spring onions, finely sliced (optional)
75 g/3 oz grated Cheddar cheese
salt and pepper
1 tablespoon olive oil

Cut the baked potatoes in half and scoop out the flesh, leaving enough round the sides for the skins to keep their shape. Mix the potato with the flaked tuna, sweetcorn, mayonnaise, milk, spring onion (if using) and 50 g/2 oz of the grated cheese, and season with a little salt and pepper. Spoon the filling back into the potato skins, top with the remaining cheese, place on a baking tray and drizzle over the olive oil. Cook for 10 minutes in an oven preheated to 180°C/350°F/ Gas 4 until golden on top.

Delicious Vegetable Rissoles ❄ ☺ ☹

Nuts and tofu are great for vegetarians as they contain many of the nutrients usually found in animal sources. Tofu and cashew nuts are both excellent sources of protein and iron.

MAKES 10 RISSOLES
150 g/5 oz grated carrot
1 medium courgette (approx. 125 g/4½ oz), topped, tailed and grated
65 g/2½ oz leek, finely chopped
1 garlic clove, crushed
200 g/7 oz chopped button mushrooms
25 g/1 oz butter
200 g/7 oz firm tofu, chopped into pieces
100 g/4 oz unsalted cashew nuts, finely chopped
100 g/4 oz fresh white breadcrumbs (made from sliced bread)
1 tablespoon soy sauce
1 tablespoon runny honey
salt and pepper
flour for coating
vegetable oil for frying

Prepare the vegetables and, using your hands, squeeze out any excess liquid from the grated carrot and courgette. Melt the butter in a frying pan and sauté the leek, garlic, carrot and courgette for 2 minutes. Add the mushrooms and cook, stirring occasionally, for 2–3 minutes.

Add the tofu, cashew nuts, breadcrumbs, soy sauce, honey and seasoning, mix well and form into 10 rissoles. Coat in flour and sauté in the oil for about 2 minutes on each side, until golden.

Confetti Couscous Salad ☺ ☹

Couscous is very tasty and you can make this in less than 10 minutes.

MAKES 1 PORTION
45 g/1½ oz couscous
125 ml/4 fl oz hot vegetable stock
20 g/1 oz red pepper, diced
½ medium carrot, peeled and diced
2 spring onions, sliced
1 tablespoon raisins
1½ tablespoons pine nuts, toasted

DRESSING
1 tablespoon olive oil
1½ teaspoons lemon juice
½ teaspoon honey
salt and pepper

Put the couscous in a bowl. Pour over the hot vegetable stock and leave to stand for about 5 minutes.

Fluff up the couscous with a fork. Stir in the diced vegetables, raisins and pine nuts.

Whisk together the ingredients for the dressing and stir into the couscous. Season to taste.

My Favourite Spanish Omelette ☺ ☹

This is good served cold and cut into wedges the next day. I give suggestions on the right for additions to the basic omelette.

MAKES 4 ADULT PORTIONS

3 tablespoons olive oil
175 g/6 oz potatoes, peeled and cut into 1 cm/½ inch cubes
1 onion, peeled and finely chopped
½ small red pepper, deseeded and chopped
50 g/2 oz frozen peas
4 eggs
2 tablespoons Parmesan cheese, grated
salt and pepper

SUGGESTED VARIATIONS

2 tablespoons Gruyère instead of Parmesan cheese
1 large chopped tomato
or
50 g/2 oz mushrooms, sliced
1 tablespoon fresh chives, snipped
or
100 g/4 oz cooked ham or bacon, cubed
50 g/2 oz sweetcorn instead of peas

Heat the oil in a non-stick 18 cm/7 inch frying pan. Fry the potato and onion for 5 minutes, then add the pepper and continue to cook for 5 minutes. Add the peas and cook for a further 5 minutes. Beat the eggs together with 1 tablespoon water and the Parmesan, and season with salt and pepper. Pour this mixture over the vegetables and cook for 5 minutes or until the omelette is almost set. To finish, brown the top under a preheated grill for about 3 minutes or until golden. (You can wrap the handle of the frying pan with silver foil to prevent it burning if necessary.) Cut into wedges and serve with salad.

Annabel's Hidden-Vegetable Tomato Sauce ❄ ☺ ☹

This is the perfect recipe for children who won't eat their vegetables, as all the vegetables are blended into the tomato sauce so they can't be identified or picked out. This tasty sauce can be used as a topping for pizzas or as a sauce for chicken and rice.

MAKES 4 ADULT PORTIONS
2 tablespoons light olive oil
1 garlic clove, crushed
1 medium onion, peeled and finely chopped
100 g/4 oz carrots, peeled and grated
50 g/2 oz courgette, grated
50 g/2 oz button mushrooms, sliced
1 teaspoon balsamic vinegar
400 g/14 oz passata (ready-sieved tomatoes)
1 teaspoon soft brown sugar
1 vegetable stock cube dissolved in 400 ml/²/₃ pint boiling water
a handful fresh basil leaves, torn
salt and freshly ground black pepper

Heat the oil in a saucepan, add the crushed garlic and sauté for a few seconds, then add the onion and sauté for a further 2 minutes. Add the carrots, courgette and mushrooms and sauté for 4 minutes, stirring occasionally. Add the balsamic vinegar and cook for 1 minute. Stir in the passata and sugar, cover and simmer for 8 minutes. Add the vegetable stock and cook for 2 minutes, stirring continuously. Add the basil and season to taste. Transfer to a blender and blitz until smooth.

Home-made Fast Food Pizza ☺ ☹

These delicious easy-to-make pizzas are always popular. If you prefer you can use crumpets, halved small baguettes or split pitta breads grilled for a minute or two as the base of the pizzas.

MAKES 2 INDIVIDUAL PIZZAS
1 English muffin, split in half
1 tablespoon good-quality tomato sauce
1 teaspoon red pesto
1 tablespoon olive oil
½ small red onion, peeled and chopped
2 button mushrooms, sliced
½ small courgette (approx. 50 g/2 oz), thinly sliced
1 slice ham or salami, cut into pieces (optional)
50 g/2 oz grated Cheddar or mozzarella cheese
salt and freshly ground black pepper

Toast the muffin until golden and leave to cool. Preheat the grill to high. Mix the passata or tomato sauce and pesto and spread over the muffins. Heat the olive oil in a frying pan and cook the onion for 2 minutes, then add the mushrooms and courgette and cook until softened and golden. Season to taste.

Divide the vegetable mixture between the muffin bases and spread over evenly. Sprinkle over the ham or salami (if using) and top with the cheese. Place under the preheated grill and cook for about 4 minutes or until golden and bubbling.

Fish

Salmon Fishcakes ❄ ☺ ☹

Salmon is a good source of omega-3 fatty acids, which are important for brain and visual development. Doctors recommend including at least two oil-rich fish dishes a week to keep the heart in good shape. These fishcakes taste good hot or cold.

MAKES 8 FISHCAKES

300 g/11 oz potatoes, peeled and cut into chunks
15 g/½ oz butter
400 g/14 oz canned red salmon, drained
½ small onion, peeled and finely chopped
2 spring onions, finely chopped
2 tablespoons tomato ketchup
salt and pepper
flour for coating
1 egg, lightly beaten
75 g/3 oz matzo meal or breadcrumbs
oil for frying

Boil the potatoes in a saucepan of lightly salted water. Drain and mash with the butter. Flake the salmon and carefully remove any bones. Mix with the mashed potato, onion, spring onions, tomato ketchup and seasoning. Form into about 8 fishcakes, coat in flour, dip in the egg and then coat in matzo meal or breadcrumbs. Heat the oil in a large frying pan and fry the fishcakes on both sides until golden.

Nursery Fish Pie ❄ ☺ ☹

MAKES 6 ADULT PORTIONS

350 g/12 oz fillet of cod skinned, or 175 g/6 oz fillets of both cod and salmon
350 ml/12 fl oz milk
1 bay leaf
4 peppercorns
a sprig of fresh parsley
salt and pepper
25 g/1 oz butter
25 g/1 oz plain flour
40 g/1½ oz grated Cheddar cheese
2 tablespoons fresh chives, snipped
½ tablespoon chopped dill (optional)
2 teaspoons lemon juice
1 hard-boiled egg, chopped
60 g/2½ oz frozen peas, cooked following packet instructions

TOPPING
550 g/1½ lb potatoes, peeled and cut into pieces
40 g/1½ oz butter
2 tablespoons milk

Put the fish in a saucepan with the milk, bay leaf, peppercorns, parsley and seasoning. Bring to the boil and then simmer, uncovered, for about 5 minutes or until the fish is cooked. Cook the potatoes for the topping in boiling, lightly salted water until soft. Drain, then mash together with 25 g/1 oz of the butter and the milk.

Drain the fish, reserving the cooking liquid. Melt the butter in a saucepan and stir in the flour. Cook gently for 1 minute, then whisk in the fish liquid gradually and bring to the boil. Simmer for 2–3 minutes until smooth, stirring continuously. Take off the heat and stir in the grated cheese until melted. Break the fish into chunks and fold in together with the chives, dill (if using), lemon juice, boiled egg, peas and seasoning. Place the fish in an ovenproof dish (an 18 cm/7 inch-diameter and 7½ cm/3 inch-deep round dish is perfect) and top with the mashed potato. Bake in the oven preheated to 180°C/350°F/Gas 4 for 15–20 minutes. Dot with the remaining butter and grill for about 2 minutes until brown and crispy.

Grandma's Tasty Fish Pie ❄ ☺ ☹

This is one of my mother's recipes and is a great favourite with all the family.
There is never any left the next day.

MAKES 6 ADULT PORTIONS

450 g/1 lb cod or haddock fillets, skinned
seasoned flour
1 egg, lightly beaten
100 g/4 oz fine breadcrumbs
vegetable oil
1 onion, peeled and finely chopped
1½ tablespoons olive oil
75 g/3 oz green pepper, cored, deseeded and chopped
150 g/5 oz red pepper, cored, deseeded and chopped
400 g/14 oz canned tomatoes
2 tablespoons tomato purée
½ teaspoon soft brown sugar
salt and pepper

CHEESE SAUCE

25 g/1 oz butter
1 tablespoon plain flour
250 ml/8 fl oz milk
75 g/3 oz Cheddar cheese, grated
40 g/1½ oz Parmesan cheese, grated

Preheat the oven to 180°C/350°F/Gas 4. Cut the fish fillets into about 12 pieces,
dip in seasoned flour, then into the lightly beaten egg, and finally coat in
breadcrumbs. Sauté in the vegetable oil until golden on both sides. Drain on
kitchen paper.

Sauté the onion in the olive oil for 3–4 minutes. Add the peppers and cook for
5 minutes. Drain half of the juice from the tomatoes, then add the tomatoes and
the remaining juice to the peppers with the tomato purée and sugar. Season

to taste and cook for about 5 minutes. Mix the cooked fish with the tomato sauce and transfer to an ovenproof dish.

Make a cheese sauce with the butter, flour and milk, stirring over a low heat until smooth and thick (see page 67). Remove from the heat and stir in two-thirds of the Cheddar and Parmesan.

Pour the cheese sauce over the fish fillets. Sprinkle with the remaining grated cheese and bake in the preheated oven for about 20 minutes. Brown under a hot grill.

Fish in Creamy Mushroom Sauce ❄ ☺ ☹

For older children, cook 225 g/8 oz fresh spinach, lay each whole fillet on a bed of spinach and pour over the sauce.

MAKES 4 ADULT PORTIONS
1 small onion, peeled and finely chopped
40 g/1½ oz butter
225 g/8 oz button mushrooms, washed and finely chopped
2 tablespoons lemon juice
2 tablespoons fresh parsley, chopped
2 tablespoons plain flour
300 ml/10 fl oz milk
1 sole or plaice, filleted

Fry the onion in half the butter until transparent. Add the mushrooms, lemon juice and parsley and cook for 2 minutes. Add the flour and cook for 2 minutes, stirring continuously. Add the milk gradually and cook, stirring continuously, until the sauce is thick and smooth.

Fry the sole fillets in the rest of the butter for 2–3 minutes on each side. Cut or flake the fish into small pieces and mix with the mushroom sauce. Alternatively, cover the uncooked fish with the mushroom sauce and bake in the oven preheated to 180°C/350°F/Gas 4 for about 15 minutes or until the fish just flakes.

Mummy's Favourite Fish Pie ✱ ☺ ☹

If you want your child to grow up liking fish then you should try this delicious fish pie. It's good to freeze individual portions in ramekin dishes for days when you don't want to cook.

MAKES 4 MINI FISH PIES

500 g/1 lb 2 oz potatoes, peeled and diced
4 tablespoons milk
75 g/3 oz butter
1 small onion, finely chopped
2 tomatoes, skinned, deseeded and chopped
1½ tablespoons flour
200 ml/7 fl oz milk
225 g/8 oz cod fillets, skinned and cut into fairly large cubes
225 g/8 oz salmon fillets, skinned and cut into fairly large cubes
1 tablespoon chopped parsley
1 bay leaf
50 g/2 oz grated Cheddar cheese
1 egg, lightly beaten
a little salt and freshly ground black pepper (for children over one)

Cook the potatoes in a pan of lightly salted water until tender (about 15 minutes), then drain and mash together with the 4 tablespoons of milk and half of the butter and season to taste.

Melt the remaining butter in a heavy-based saucepan and sauté the onion for 3 minutes. Add the chopped tomatoes and sauté for 2–3 minutes. Stir in the flour and cook for 1 minute. Add the milk, bring to the boil and cook for 1 minute. Stir in the cod, salmon, parsley and bay leaf and simmer for 3–4 minutes. Remove the bay leaf, stir in the grated Cheddar until melted and season to taste.

Preheat the oven to 180°C/350°F/Gas 4. Divide the fish between 4 ramekin dishes (about 8–10 cm/4 inches in diameter) and top with the mashed potato. Brush the potato with lightly beaten egg and bake in the oven for 15–20 minutes. You can brown them under a preheated grill for a few minutes at the end if you wish.

Kids' Kedgeree ❄ ☺ ☹

This really scrummy kedgeree makes a great family meal that is popular with kids. It's the kind of food you could eat for breakfast or supper. If you want to make a smaller amount, simply halve the quantities.

MAKES 6 ADULT PORTIONS
350 g/12 oz undyed smoked haddock
100 ml/3½ fl oz double cream
25 g/1 oz butter
1 onion, peeled and chopped
1 teaspoon mild curry paste
200 g/7 oz basmati rice, cooked
1 teaspoon lemon juice
2 tablespoons fresh parsley, chopped
2 hard-boiled eggs, chopped
salt and pepper

Place the haddock in a microwave-proof dish and pour over the cream. Cover with clingfilm, pierce a few times with the tip of a sharp knife and place in the microwave on High for 5–6 minutes. Meanwhile, in a frying pan or wok, melt the butter and sauté the onion for 8 minutes until soft. Stir in the curry paste and rice and cook for 1 minute, stirring continuously. Flake in the haddock and add the cooking liquor, lemon juice, parsley and chopped eggs. Season with salt and pepper if necessary.

Toasted Tuna Muffins ❄ ☺ ☹

A can of tuna in the larder is a good standby and tuna is rich in protein, Vitamin D and Vitamin B12. These toasted muffins are quick and easy to make for a tasty and healthy meal.

MAKES 1–2 PORTIONS
100 g/4 oz canned tuna in oil, drained
1 tablespoon crème fraîche or mayonnaise
1 tablespoon tomato ketchup
1 spring onion, finely chopped
2 tablespoons canned sweetcorn
1 English muffin
25 g/1 oz grated Cheddar cheese

Flake the tuna into a bowl and stir in the mayonnaise, tomato ketchup, spring onion and sweetcorn. Preheat the grill, divide the muffin into 2 halves and toast. Divide the tuna mixture between the 2 halves. Cover with the grated cheese and place under the grill for about 2 minutes until golden and bubbling.

Tuna Pitta Pockets ☺ ☹

MAKES 2 PITTA POCKETS
100 g/4 oz canned tuna in oil, drained
50 g/2 oz sweetcorn
1 hard-boiled egg, chopped
1 tablespoon mayonnaise
½ teaspoon white wine vinegar
2 spring onions, chopped
1 tomato, skinned, deseeded and chopped
salt and freshly ground black pepper
1 pitta bread

Flake the tuna with a fork and mix with the sweetcorn, hard-boiled egg, mayonnaise, white wine vinegar, spring onions, tomato and seasoning. Toast the pitta bread, cut in half to make two pockets and divide the mixture between them.

Tuna Tagliatelle ❄ ☺ ☹

MAKES 6 ADULT PORTIONS

½ onion, peeled and finely chopped
25 g/1 oz butter
1 tablespoon cornflour
120 ml/4 fl oz water
400 g/14 oz canned cream of tomato soup
a pinch of mixed dried herbs
1 tablespoon fresh parsley, chopped
200 g/7 oz canned tuna, drained and flaked
black pepper
175 g/6 oz green tagliatelle
1 tablespoon grated Parmesan cheese

MUSHROOM CHEESE SAUCE

½ onion, peeled and finely chopped
40 g/1½ oz butter
100 g/4 oz mushrooms, washed and sliced
2 tablespoons plain flour
300 ml/10 fl oz milk
100 g/4 oz Cheddar cheese, grated

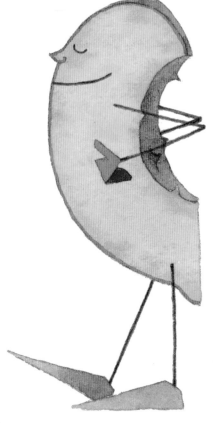

For the sauce, fry the onion in the butter until transparent, then add the sliced mushrooms and sauté for about 3 minutes. Add the flour and continue stirring the mixture all the time. When it is well mixed, add the milk gradually and cook, stirring until thickened and smooth. Remove from the heat and stir in the grated cheese.

Fry the onion in the butter until soft. Stir the cornflour into the water until dissolved, mix with the tomato soup then add to the onion. Add the mixed dried herbs and fresh parsley and cook, stirring, over a low heat for 5 minutes. Mix in the flaked tuna and heat through. Season with a little black pepper.

Boil the tagliatelle in water until al dente, then drain. Grease a serving dish and add the tuna and tomato mixed with the pasta and then the mushroom cheese sauce. Top with grated Parmesan. Bake in an oven preheated to 180°C/350°F/Gas 4 for 20 minutes. Brown under a hot grill before serving.

Tuna with Pasta and Tomatoes ☺ ☺

The red onion and sunblush tomatoes give this pasta dish a lovely flavour.
Sunblush tomatoes are sweet, semi-dried tomatoes, and are not as hard
as normal sun-dried tomatoes.

MAKES 4 PORTIONS

200 g/7 oz penne
2 tablespoons olive oil
1 medium red onion, peeled and finely sliced
4 ripe plum tomatoes, quartered, deseeded and roughly chopped
200 g/7 oz canned tuna in oil, drained
75 g/3 oz sunblush tomatoes, chopped
1 teaspoon balsamic vinegar
a handful of fresh basil leaves, torn
salt and freshly ground black pepper

Cook the penne in boiling salted water according to the packet instructions.
Meanwhile, heat the oil in a frying pan, add the onion and cook for about
6 minutes, stirring occasionally until softened. Stir in the fresh tomatoes
and cook for 2–3 minutes until beginning to soften. Add the tuna, sunblush
tomatoes, balsamic vinegar, basil and seasoning and cook for 1 minute before
stirring into the pasta and serving.

Thai-Style Chicken and Noodles ❄ ☺ ☹

Don't be afraid to try out new tastes on your child – this recipe flavoured with mild curry and coconut sauce is very popular. Young children often surprise us and like quite sophisticated foods and it's usually easier to get children to accept new tastes whilst they are young. This would make a good meal for the whole family.

MAKES 4 PORTIONS

MARINADE

1 tablespoon soy sauce
1 tablespoon sake
½ teaspoon sugar
1 teaspoon cornflour

1½ chicken breasts cut into strips
125 g/4½ oz Chinese noodles
1 tablespoon vegetable oil
3 spring onions, sliced
1 garlic clove, crushed
½ teaspoon red chilli, deseeded and chopped
1½–2 teaspoons korma curry paste
150 ml/5 fl oz chicken stock (see page 76)
150 ml/5 fl oz coconut milk
75 g/3 oz baby corn cobs, cut into quarters
100 g/4 oz beansprouts
75 g/3 oz frozen peas

Mix together the ingredients for the marinade and marinate the chicken for at least 30 minutes. Cook the noodles according to the packet instructions, drain and rinse under cold water. Heat the vegetable oil in a wok or frying pan and stir-fry the spring onions, garlic and chilli for about 2 minutes. Drain the marinade from the chicken, add to the wok and continue to stir-fry for 2 minutes. Add the curry paste, chicken stock and coconut milk and cook for 5 minutes over a low heat. Add the baby corn and beansprouts and cook for 3–4 minutes. Add the peas and cook for 2 minutes more. Add the noodles to the pan to heat through.

Bar-B-Q Chicken ☺ ☹

A good marinade will transform your barbecue, tenderising the meat, as well as adding a delicious flavour. I use a Weber Bar-B-Q, which has a cover, enabling me to barbecue all year round, even in England. Use 900 g/2 lb breast of chicken, skinned and on the bone, with these marinades – they also work well with beef or lamb.

MAKES 4–5 ADULT PORTIONS

HOISIN MARINADE

2 tablespoons soy sauce
2 tablespoons hoisin sauce
2 tablespoons rice wine vinegar
1 tablespoon honey
1 tablespoon vegetable oil
½ teaspoon crushed garlic (optional)

TERIYAKI MARINADE

3 tablespoons rice wine vinegar or white wine vinegar
2 tablespoons soy sauce
1 tablespoon honey
½ tablespoon sesame oil
1 teaspoon grated ginger root (optional)
1 tablespoon sliced spring onion

Mix all the marinade ingredients together. Marinate the chicken for at least 2 hours, then barbecue, basting and turning occasionally for 15–25 minutes. Dark meat takes longer to cook than white meat. Chicken should be cooked through, but not overcooked or it will become dry. If you are unsure about cooking meat thoroughly before the surface is charred, cook it in an oven preheated to 200°C/400°F/Gas 6 for 25–30 minutes and finish it on the barbecue for a few minutes to give an authentic flavour.

Chicken Satay ☺ ☹

These barbecued chicken skewers are fun to eat and very popular with toddlers. Help your child take the meat off the skewers, then remove the skewers – they could become dangerous in the hands of exuberant children.

MAKES 2 ADULT PORTIONS
2 chicken breasts, off the bone
1 small onion, peeled
1 small red pepper, deseeded

MARINADE
2 tablespoons peanut butter
1 tablespoon chicken stock (see page 76)
1 tablespoon rice wine vinegar
1 tablespoon honey
1 tablespoon soy sauce
1 teaspoon crushed garlic (optional)
1 teaspoon sesame seeds, toasted (optional)

Mix together the marinade ingredients. Soak 4 bamboo skewers in water to prevent them getting scorched. Cut the chicken, onion and pepper into chunks. Leave the chicken in the marinade for at least 2 hours. Thread with the onion and pepper onto the skewers (or just use chicken). Cook under a preheated grill for about 5 minutes each side, basting occasionally. Alternatively, cook on a barbecue or griddle.

Chicken Soup with Pasta and Vegetables ❄ ☺ ☹

This is a quick and easy chicken noodle soup that is very popular with my three children. Vermicelli is fine pasta that comes rolled up in nests.

MAKES 6 PORTIONS

1 litre/1¾ pints chicken stock
1 tablespoon vegetable oil
1 onion, peeled and thinly sliced
1 garlic clove, crushed
125 g/4½ oz chicken breast, cut into bite-sized pieces
¼ teaspoon chicken seasoning
50 g/2 oz green beans, topped, tailed and cut into short lengths
50 g/2 oz vermicelli or tiny pasta stars
1 tomato, skinned, deseeded and chopped

Make up the chicken stock in a pan using either 2 chicken stock cubes and boiling water, liquid stock from a supermarket or my recipe on page 76. Meanwhile, heat the vegetable oil in another saucepan and sauté the onion and garlic for 2 minutes. Add the chicken, sprinkle with chicken seasoning and sauté for 1 minute, stirring occasionally, then add the green beans and sauté for 3 minutes. Mix the chicken, onion, green beans and vermicelli with the chicken stock. Bring to the boil, then reduce the heat and cook for 3–4 minutes or until the pasta is cooked and the beans are just tender. Stir in the chopped tomato and cook for 1 minute.

Marinated Chicken on the Griddle ☺ ☹

I enjoy cooking chicken, meat or fish on a griddle, and it's a really healthy way of cooking as it uses very little fat. My three children love this recipe as marinating the chicken gives it a lovely flavour and makes it more tender. Make sure the griddle is really hot before you lay the food on it.

MAKES 2 ADULT PORTIONS
2 boneless chicken breasts
1 tablespoon olive oil

MARINADE
1 tablespoon lemon juice
1 tablespoon soy sauce
1 tablespoon honey
1 small garlic clove, peeled and sliced
2 sprigs of fresh rosemary (optional)

Score the chicken breasts 2 or 3 times with a sharp knife. Season with salt and pepper. Mix together all the ingredients for the marinade and marinate the chicken for at least 2 hours. Heat the griddle, brush with oil, then remove the chicken from the marinade and cook for 4–5 minutes on each side or until cooked through. Cut into strips and serve with colourful vegetables such as carrots, broccoli or peas, and chips or mashed potato.

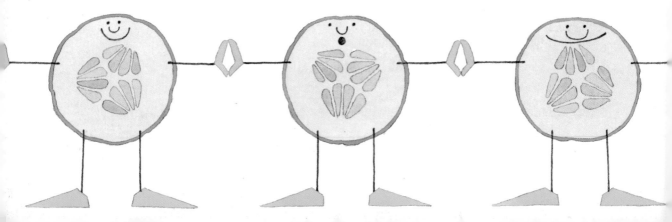

Mulligatawny Chicken ❄ ☺ ☹

This recipe has a tomato base and a mild curry flavour that children love. It has been a family favourite since I was a child and was invented by my mother. It is best served with rice and, for special occasions, you can serve poppadoms as an accompaniment. They are available in most supermarkets.

MAKES 8 ADULT PORTIONS

1 chicken, cut into about 10 pieces, skinned
seasoned flour
vegetable oil
2 medium onions, peeled and chopped
6 tablespoons tomato purée
2 tablespoons mild curry powder
900 ml/1½ pints chicken stock (see page 76)
1 large or 2 small apples, cored and thinly sliced
1 small carrot, peeled and thinly sliced
2 lemon slices
75 g/3 oz sultanas
1 bay leaf
1 dessertspoon brown sugar
salt and pepper

Coat the chicken pieces with seasoned flour. Fry in vegetable oil until golden brown. Drain on kitchen paper and place in a casserole dish.

Fry the onion in a little oil until golden, then stir in the tomato purée. Add the curry powder and continue to stir for a couple of minutes over a low heat. Stir in 2 tablespoons of flour, then pour in 300 ml/10 fl oz of the stock, mixing well.

Add the apple, carrot, lemon slices, sultanas, bay leaf and the rest of the stock. Season with brown sugar, salt and pepper. Pour the sauce over the chicken in the casserole, cover and cook for 1 hour in an oven preheated to 180°C/350°F/Gas 4. Remove the lemon slices and bay leaf; take the chicken off the bone and cut it into pieces.

Sesame Chicken Nuggets
with Chinese Sauce ❄ ☺ ☹

These crisp sesame-coated nuggets in a tasty sauce are very popular. They are good served with Special Fried Rice (see page 150). It's fun for children to eat these with chopsticks – you can buy plastic chopsticks that are joined together at the top and are very easy for children to use. Sesame seeds can cause an allergic reaction in young children. Although this is very rare, watch your child closely, particularly if he is allergic to any other foods, or has any conditions such as eczema or asthma.

MAKES 12 NUGGETS

2 chicken breasts, off the bone and skinned
1 egg
1 tablespoon milk
seasoned flour
100 g/4 oz sesame seeds
2 tablespoons vegetable oil

CHINESE SAUCE

250 ml/8 fl oz unsalted chicken stock (see page 76)
2 teaspoons soy sauce
1 teaspoon sesame oil
1 tablespoon caster sugar
1 teaspoon cider vinegar
1 tablespoon cornflour
1 spring onion, finely sliced

Cut each chicken breast into about six pieces. Beat the egg together with the milk and dip the nuggets into seasoned flour, then into the egg and finally coat with sesame seeds. Fry in hot oil for about 5 minutes, turning the chicken frequently, until golden brown and cooked through. Mix together all the ingredients for the sauce, apart from the spring onion, in a small saucepan. Bring to the boil and then simmer for 2–3 minutes or until thickened. Add the spring onion and pour the sauce over the chicken.

Red meats

Annabel's Tasty Beefburgers ❄ ☺ ☹

The grated apple makes these beefburgers really moist and tasty. Serve in a bun with salad and ketchup, and some oven-baked chips. They are also good cooked on a barbecue in summer. If you want to freeze burgers it's best to freeze them uncooked on a tray lined with cling film. Then, when frozen, wrap each one individually in cling film so that you can remove and defrost them as and when you need them.

MAKES 8 BURGERS

½ red pepper, cored, deseeded and chopped
1 onion, peeled and finely chopped
1 tablespoon vegetable oil
450 g/1 lb lean minced beef or lamb
1 tablespoon fresh parsley, chopped
1 chicken stock cube, finely crumbled
1 apple, peeled and grated
1 egg, lightly beaten
25 g/1 oz fresh breadcrumbs
1 teaspoon Worcestershire sauce
salt and freshly ground black pepper
a little plain flour
vegetable oil for brushing a griddle pan or for frying

Fry the red pepper and half the onion in the vegetable oil for about 5 minutes or until softened. In a mixing bowl, combine the sautéed onion, pepper and remaining raw onion with all the ingredients except for the flour and vegetable oil. With floured hands, form into 8 burgers. Brush a griddle pan with a little oil and, when hot, place 4 burgers on the griddle and cook for about 5 minutes each side or until browned and cooked through. Repeat with the remaining burgers. Alternatively, fry in a little hot oil in a shallow frying pan. Serve the burgers on their own or in a toasted hamburger bun with salad and ketchup.

Cocktail Meatballs with Tomato Sauce ❄ ☺ ☹

MAKES 6 PORTIONS

TOMATO SAUCE
1½ tablespoons light olive oil
1 medium onion, peeled and chopped
1 garlic clove, crushed
250 g/9 oz fresh ripe tomatoes, skinned, deseeded and chopped
400 g/14 oz canned tomatoes, chopped
1 teaspoon balsamic vinegar
1 teaspoon caster sugar
salt and freshly ground black pepper
1 tablespoon fresh basil, torn

MEATBALLS
350 g/12 oz lean minced beef
1 medium onion, peeled and finely chopped
1 Granny Smith apple, peeled and grated
50 g/2 oz fresh white breadcrumbs
1 tablespoon fresh parsley, chopped
1 chicken stock cube, finely crumbled and dissolved in 2 tablespoons boiling water
salt and freshly ground black pepper
plain flour for forming meatballs
vegetable oil for frying

To make the tomato sauce, heat the oil in a saucepan and gently cook the onion and garlic until softened. Stir in the fresh tomatoes and cook for 1 minute. Add the canned tomatoes, vinegar, sugar and seasoning and cook for 20 minutes over a low heat. Add the basil and then blend in a food processor to make a smooth sauce.

Meanwhile, mix together the ingredients for the meatballs. Using floured hands, form into about 24 balls. Heat the oil in a frying pan and sauté the meatballs over a fairly high heat, turning occasionally, until browned, then reduce the heat and continue to cook for about 5 minutes. Pour over the tomato sauce and continue to cook, covered, for 10–15 minutes.

Mini Minute Steaks ☺ ☹

These mini steaks with a full-flavoured gravy and sautéed potatoes are absolutely delicious.

MAKES 2 ADULT OR 4 CHILD PORTIONS
2 tablespoons vegetable oil
1 onion, peeled and thinly sliced
1 teaspoon caster sugar
1 tablespoon water
200 ml/7 fl oz beef stock
1 teaspoon cornflour mixed with
1 tablespoon water
a few drops of Worcestershire sauce
1 teaspoon tomato purée
salt and pepper
350 g/12 oz peeled potatoes
25 g/1 oz butter
4 x 60 g/2½ oz minute steaks (fillet or rump), about 5 mm/¼ inch thick

To make the gravy, heat 1 tablespoon of the vegetable oil in a frying pan. Add the onion and cook for 7–8 minutes until just turning golden brown. Stir in the sugar and water, increase the heat and cook for about 1 minute until the water has evaporated. Stir in the beef stock, cornflour mixed with 1 tablespoon water, Worcestershire sauce and tomato purée. Season with salt and pepper. Cook, stirring, for 2–3 minutes until thickened.

For the sautéed potatoes, cut the potatoes into large chunks, bring to the boil in lightly salted water and cook for about 8 minutes until they are just tender. Drain and cut into 1 cm/½ inch-thick slices. Heat the butter in a frying pan and sauté the potatoes for 5–6 minutes, turning occasionally until golden brown and crispy.

Heat the remaining oil in a frying pan, season the steaks and fry for 1–2 minutes each side. Serve with the gravy and sautéed potatoes.

Shredded Beef with Broccoli ❄ ☺ ☹

A quick and easy-to-prepare beef stir-fry with a tasty sauce. To toast sesame seeds, stir-fry them in a dry frying pan for a couple of minutes until golden, stirring to make sure that they don't burn.

MAKES 4 ADULT PORTIONS

175 g/6 oz rice
1 tablespoon sesame oil
½ tablespoon sunflower oil
1 onion, peeled and chopped
1 garlic clove, crushed
1 medium carrot, peeled and cut into matchsticks
100 g/4 oz broccoli florets
250 g/9 oz beef fillet, cut into fine strips
1 tablespoon cornflour
150 ml/5 fl oz beef stock
2 tablespoons dark brown sugar
1½ tablespoons soy sauce
1 tablespoon toasted sesame seeds

Cook the rice according to the packet instructions. Heat the sesame oil and sunflower oil in a wok or frying pan and stir-fry the onion and garlic for 3–4 minutes. Add the carrot and broccoli and stir-fry for 2 minutes. Add the beef strips and stir-fry for 4–5 minutes. Mix the cornflour with 1 tablespoon of cold water and stir into the beef stock. Stir this into the pan, together with the sugar, soy sauce and toasted sesame seeds. Bring to a simmer and cook for 2 minutes. Serve with the cooked rice.

Spaghetti with Two-Tomato Sauce ❄ ☺ ☹

A really good home-made tomato sauce is always popular – it can be served with any type of pasta and maybe freshly grated Parmesan cheese.

MAKES 4 PORTIONS

3 tablespoons olive oil
1 onion, peeled and chopped
1 garlic clove, peeled and crushed
4 ripe tomatoes, skinned, deseeded and chopped
400 g/14 oz canned tomatoes, chopped
a pinch of sugar
1 bay leaf
2 tablespoons fresh basil, chopped
salt and pepper
250 g/9 oz spaghetti

Heat the oil in a saucepan and sauté the onion and garlic for 5–6 minutes until softened. Add the fresh and canned tomatoes, sugar, bay leaf and chopped basil, then season with salt and pepper. Bring to a simmer and cook for 20 minutes. Meanwhile, cook the spaghetti according to the packet instructions. Drain the pasta and mix with the sauce.

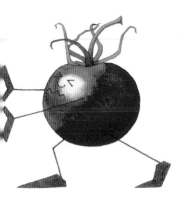

Bow-Ties with Gruyère and Cherry Tomatoes ☺ ☹

A great favourite with my children, this can be eaten either warm or cold.

MAKES 4 PORTIONS
175 g/6 oz bow-tie pasta
1 tablespoon white wine vinegar
3 tablespoons olive oil
½ teaspoon Dijon mustard (optional)
a pinch of sugar
a little salt and freshly ground black pepper
1 tablespoon fresh chives, snipped
100 g/4 oz cherry tomatoes, halved or quartered
50 g/2 oz Gruyère cheese, grated

Cook the pasta in lightly salted water according to the packet instructions. Make a vinaigrette by mixing together the vinegar, oil, mustard (if using), sugar and seasoning, then add the snipped chives. Drain the pasta and put into a bowl, then mix with the cherry tomatoes and grated Gruyère cheese. Shake the vinaigrette, pour over the pasta and toss well to coat.

Three Cheese Sauce ❄ ☺ ☹

This makes a really delicious, creamy cheese sauce for pasta. If you like you can add a couple of slices of good-quality cooked ham, shredded.

MAKES 4 PORTIONS
30 g/1 oz butter
30 g/1 oz flour
300 ml/11 fl oz milk
50 g/2 oz Gruyère cheese, grated
40 g/1½ oz Parmesan cheese, grated
150 g/5 oz mascarpone cheese

Melt the butter, stir in the flour and cook for 1 minute. Gradually add the milk, then continue to stir for 5 minutes over a low heat until the sauce thickens. Remove from the heat, stir in the Gruyère and Parmesan cheeses until melted, then stir in the mascarpone.

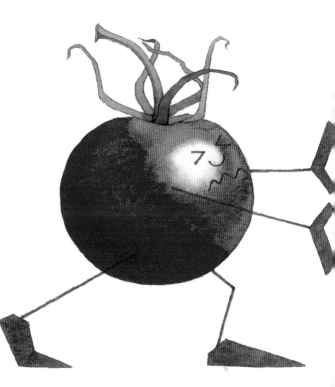

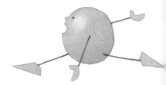

Spaghetti Primavera ❄ ☺ ☹

A simple recipe for spaghetti with spring vegetables in a tasty cheese sauce.
You could also make this with pasta shapes.

MAKES 4 PORTIONS
150 g/5 oz spaghetti
1 tablespoon olive oil
1 onion, chopped
1 garlic clove, crushed
1 medium carrot (approx. 75 g/3 oz) cut into matchsticks
1 medium courgette (approx. 75 g/3 oz) cut into matchsticks
125 g/4½ oz cauliflower cut into small florets
150 ml/5 fl oz light crème fraîche
150 ml/5 fl oz vegetable stock (see page 38)
50 g/2 oz frozen peas
50 g/2 oz fresh Parmesan cheese, grated

Cook the spaghetti according to the packet instructions. At the same time
heat the oil in a heavy-bottomed saucepan and sauté the onion and garlic
for 1 minute. Add the carrot and courgette matchsticks and sauté, stirring
occasionally, for 2–3 minutes. Meanwhile, blanch the cauliflower in lightly
salted boiling water for 5 minutes or steam until tender. Add the crème fraîche,
vegetable stock and peas to the carrot and courgette and stir in. Cook for
2–3 minutes before stirring in the Parmesan. Drain the spaghetti and toss
with the sauce.

Fruit

Apple and Blackberry Crumble ❄ ☺ ☹

A really good crumble bursting with fruit is comfort food at its very best and very easy to prepare. I think fruits with a slightly tart flavour are best in a crumble. A good combination is 400 g/1 lb rhubarb, thinly sliced and mixed with 100 g/4 oz strawberries and 4 tablespoons of caster sugar – this doesn't need any pre-cooking. You could also make this in individual ramekins. Sprinkling the dish with the ground almonds ensures some of the liquid is absorbed, so that it doesn't bubble over the top. You don't need to do this if using small ramekins.

MAKES 6 PORTIONS
40 g/1½ oz butter
750 g/1 lb 11 oz eating apples (e.g. Gala, Pink Lady), peeled, cored and chopped
2½ tablespoons soft brown sugar
350 g/12 oz blackberries, fresh or frozen
2 tablespoons ground almonds (if using one large dish)

CRUMBLE TOPPING
150 g/5 oz plain flour
a generous pinch of salt
100 g/4 oz cold butter, cut into cubes
85 g/3½ oz demerara sugar
25 g/1 oz porridge oats

Melt the butter in a large pan and sauté the chopped apples with the sugar for 3–4 minutes, stirring occasionally. Finally, stir in the blackberries.

Sprinkle the base of a 20 cm/8 inch round, glass ovenproof dish with the ground almonds. This helps to soak up some of the juices. Spoon the fruit over the top. Alternatively, make individual portions and spoon the fruit into six 10 cm/3½ inch ramekin dishes. The ramekins will seem quite full but the fruit will reduce down as it cooks.

To make the topping, whiz the flour, salt, butter and sugar in a food processor and then stir in the porridge oats. Alternatively, mix together the flour, salt and sugar, and then rub in the butter using your fingers; stir in the porridge oats.

Preheat the oven to 180°C/350°F/Gas 4. Sprinkle the crumble topping over the fruit and bake in the oven for 35 minutes.

Mini-Cheesecakes ❄ ☺ ☹

Really simple and quick to prepare, these individual mini-cheesecakes are made in muffin cases and don't need any baking. Everyone in my family thinks they are yummy. Great for a tea party or birthday celebration. They are also fun for children to make themselves. If you don't want to make these in paper cases you could also make them in small glass ramekins.

MAKES 6 MINI-CHEESECAKES

6 digestive biscuits
50 g/2 oz butter
1 x 250 g/9 oz tub mascarpone cheese
6 tablespoons lemon curd
1 tablespoon lemon juice
120 ml/4 fl oz double cream
3 teaspoons lemon curd (optional)

Line a muffin tray with 6 large paper cases. Put the biscuits in a bag and crush them into crumbs using a rolling pin. Melt the butter and stir in the crumbs. Divide the crumbs between the muffin cases and use clean fingers to press firmly into the base. Chill in the fridge whilst you prepare the filling.

Beat together the mascarpone cheese, lemon curd and lemon juice in an electric mixer. Whip the cream until it just holds its shape (soft peaks). Fold the cream into the cheese mixture. Spoon the filling into the paper cases. If you like you can top each one with half a teaspoon of lemon curd and swirl this with a cocktail stick to make a pattern.

Annabel's Bread and Butter Pudding ☺ ☹

This is the perfect pudding for when the cupboard is pretty bare. It is also delicious made with raisin bread, cholla or sliced panettone cake.

MAKES 4 ADULT PORTIONS

30 g/1½ oz butter at room temperature, plus extra for greasing
4 slices white bread, crusts removed
2 tablespoons apricot jam
50 g/2 oz raisins
250 ml/8 fl oz double cream
250 ml/8 fl oz milk
1 teaspoon vanilla extract
2 large eggs plus yolk of 1 egg
50 g/2 oz caster sugar

Preheat the oven to 160°C/325°F/Gas 3. Spread a thin layer of butter on the bread, then spread on the apricot jam. Cut the bread into triangles. Lightly butter a 21 x 16 x 6 cm(approx. 1.5 litres) rectangular baking dish. Arrange the slices of bread in the baking dish and scatter over the raisins. Whisk together the cream, milk, vanilla, eggs and sugar and pour this over the bread. The bread should not be completely covered but should stick up out of the cream mixture so that the top becomes crisp. Put the baking dish in a large roasting tin and pour boiling water to halfway up the dish. Bake for 40–45 minutes.

Ice Lollies

Make up your own flavours. Experiment with different combinations like puréed and strained fresh or frozen berries sweetened with a little icing sugar and mixed with cranberry or blackcurrant juice. You can also mix in some yoghurt such as mini-probiotic drinking yoghurts. Try blending a tin of lychees with a little lemon or lime juice and sieve for a refreshing ice lolly.

Strawberry Sorbet Lollies ❄ ☺ ☹

If there is one food that no child can resist it's an ice lolly. Most shop-bought lollies are full of artificial flavouring and colouring so it's much better to make your own from fresh fruit. Strawberries contain higher levels of vitamin C than any other berries. Two-tone ice lollies are fun. Half-fill the moulds with the strawberry sorbet, freeze for a couple of hours and then pour over an orange-coloured juice like apple and mango or tropical fruit juice.

MAKES 4 ICE LOLLIES
30 g/1½ oz caster sugar
40 ml/1¾ fl oz water
250 g/9 oz strawberries, hulled and cut in half
juice of 1 medium orange (approx. 40 ml/1¾ fl oz)

Put the sugar and water into a saucepan and boil until syrupy (about 3 minutes). Allow to cool. Purée the strawberries with an electric hand blender and combine with the cooled syrup and orange juice, then pour this mixture into ice lolly moulds. Freeze until solid.

Peach and Passion Fruit Lollies ❄ ☺ ☹

Choose passion fruit with wrinkled skins as these are ripe and have the sweetest flavour.

MAKES 6 ICE LOLLIES
juice of 2 large oranges
strained juice of 3 passion fruit
2 ripe juicy peaches, skinned, stoned and chopped
icing sugar to taste

Combine all the ingredients in a blender and blend until smooth. Pour into ice lolly moulds and freeze.

Grandma's Lokshen Pudding ☺ ☹

Lokshen is vermicelli: very fine egg noodles.

MAKES 4 ADULT PORTIONS
225 g/8 oz vermicelli
1 large egg, beaten
25 g/1 oz butter, melted
250 ml/8 fl oz milk
1 tablespoon vanilla sugar or caster sugar
½ teaspoon mixed spice
75 g/3 oz each sultanas and raisins
a few flaked almonds (optional)

Cook the vermicelli in boiling water for about 5 minutes. Drain and mix with the remaining ingredients. Place in a greased, shallow baking dish, and bake in an oven preheated to 180°C/350°F/Gas 4 for about 30 minutes.

Frozen Strawberry Yoghurt Ice Cream ☺ ☹

A delicious easy-to-make frozen-yoghurt ice cream using only natural ingredients. You can also make a peach melba frozen yoghurt using fresh raspberries, puréed and strained, and peach yoghurt. I like to serve this as a Knickerbocker Glory in a tall glass with fresh berries.

MAKES 6 ADULT PORTIONS
100 g/4 oz caster sugar
300 ml/10 fl oz water
350 g/12 oz fresh strawberries
300 ml/10 fl oz strawberry yoghurt
150 ml/5 fl oz double cream, whipped
1 egg white, whisked

Put the sugar in a saucepan with the water, bring to the boil and continue to boil for 5 minutes to make a syrup. Set aside to cool for a few minutes. Purée the strawberries and press through a sieve, then mix with the syrup and stir in the yoghurt and whipped cream. Churn for 10 minutes in an ice cream-making machine, then fold in the whipped egg white and churn for another 10 minutes or until firm.

This can also be made without an ice cream machine but it will be more time-consuming. Pour the mixture into a freezerproof plastic container and freeze. Remove and whisk when semi-frozen, then return to the freezer. Whisk again after 1 hour, fold in the whipped egg white, freeze again and whisk twice more during the freezing process.

Apple Flowers ☺ ☹

You can use ready-rolled sheets of puff pastry, which only need to be unrolled
and baked – so it couldn't be simpler to make these delicious pastries.
Alternatively, use a block of puff pastry and roll it out yourself.

MAKES 6 MINI APPLE TARTS
300 g/11 oz puff pastry
40 g/1½ oz butter
40 g/1½ oz caster sugar
1 egg
a few drops of almond essence
50 g/2 oz ground almonds
25 g/1 oz melted butter
3 small eating apples
caster sugar for sprinkling
2 tablespoons apricot jam, strained
1 tablespoon lemon juice
6 glacé cherries

Preheat the oven to 200°C/400°F/Gas 6. Cut 6 circles out of the pastry using a
round pastry cutter (approx. 10 cm/4 inches) or cut around a plate using a sharp
knife. To make the almond filling, cream together the butter and sugar until soft,
then beat in the egg, a few drops of almond essence and the ground almonds to
make a smooth cream. Prick the pastry a few times with a fork and brush with
a little melted butter. Spread some of the almond cream over each of the circles.

Peel and core the apples, then cut in half and slice thinly. Arrange the sliced
fruit around the pastry circles. Brush with a little melted butter, sprinkle over
some caster sugar and bake in the preheated oven for about 20 minutes or until
the pastry is crisp and the fruit is cooked. Transfer the tarts to a wire rack to cool.

Warm the jam and lemon juice in a small saucepan and then brush the fruit
with a little of the melted, strained apricot jam to glaze the tarts. Decorate the
centre of each tart with a glacé cherry.

Carrot and Pineapple Muffins ☺ ☹

These are absolutely delicious, and very healthy too; they never last long in our house!

MAKES ABOUT 13 MUFFINS

100 g/4 oz plain flour
100 g/4 oz plain wholemeal flour
1 teaspoon baking powder
³/4 teaspoon bicarbonate of soda
1 teaspoon ground cinnamon
1 teaspoon ground ginger
½ teaspoon salt
175 ml/6 fl oz vegetable oil
75 g/3 oz caster sugar
2 eggs
125 g/4½ oz grated carrots
225 g/8 oz canned crushed pineapple, drained
100 g/4 oz raisins

Preheat the oven to 180°C/350°F/Gas 4. Sift together the flours, baking powder, bicarbonate of soda, cinnamon, ginger and salt and mix well. Beat the oil, sugar and eggs together until well blended. Add the grated carrots, crushed pineapple and raisins. Gradually add the flour mixture, beating just enough to combine all the ingredients.

Pour the batter into muffin trays lined with paper cases and bake for about 25 minutes or until golden. (These can be cooked in fairy-cake trays, but you will need to reduce the cooking time.) Cool on a wire rack.

Animal Cupcakes ❄ ☺ ☹

Fairy cakes are always popular and children will have fun decorating them to look like animals. To make chocolate cupcakes (for 'hedgehogs' or 'dogs'!) substitute 25 g/1 oz cocoa for 25 g/1 oz of the self-raising flour and use the chocolate icing.

MAKES 10 CAKES
140 g/5 oz softened butter or margarine
140 g/5 oz golden caster sugar
3 eggs
1 teaspoon pure vanilla extract
125 g/4½ oz self-raising flour

GLACÉ ICING
225 g/8 oz icing sugar, sieved
about 2½ tablespoons warm water
a few drops of food colouring

CHOCOLATE ICING
60 g/2½ oz milk chocolate
60 g/2½ oz softened butter
85 g/3½ oz icing sugar, sieved

DECORATION
Assorted sweets e.g. Liquorice Allsorts, Jelly Tots, wine gums, M&Ms, liquorice laces, chocolate flakes, black writing icing and mini-marshmallows (for sheep)

Preheat the oven to 190°C/375°F/Gas 5. Line a bun or muffin tray with 10 paper cases. Put all the ingredients for the cakes into a mixing bowl and beat for about 2 minutes until smooth. Divide the mixture between the cases so they are filled two-thirds of the way up. Bake for 18–20 minutes until risen and lightly golden.

   To make the glacé icing, mix the icing sugar with enough warm water to make a spreading consistency, then divide into three before you stir in the various colourings. Use sweets and the black writing icing to decorate.

   For the chocolate icing, break the chocolate into pieces and microwave on high for 1–2 minutes until melted, or melt in a bowl set over a pan of simmering water. Cream the butter and sugar together, then beat in the chocolate and spread on the cakes. Decorate with chocolate flakes to look like hedgehogs.

White-Chocolate-Button Cookies ❄ ☺ ☹

These are so easy to make and are really delicious. Baked for only 12 minutes, they should be quite soft when they are taken out of the oven so that when they cool down they are lovely and moist.

MAKES 20 COOKIES

100 g/4 oz unsalted butter or margarine at room temperature
100 g/4 oz caster sugar
100 g/4 oz brown sugar
1 egg
1 teaspoon vanilla essence
175 g/6 oz plain flour
½ teaspoon baking powder
¼ teaspoon salt
175 g/6 oz white chocolate buttons
75 g/3 oz pecans or walnuts, chopped (optional)

Beat the butter or margarine together with the sugars. With a fork, beat the egg together with the vanilla and add this to the butter mixture.

In a bowl, mix together the flour, baking powder and salt. Add this to the butter and egg mixture and blend well.

Break the chocolate buttons into smaller pieces with a rolling pin or in a food processor, and stir these, together with the nuts (if using), into the mixture.

Line several baking sheets with non-stick baking paper and roll the dough into walnut-sized balls. Put these onto the sheets, spaced well apart, and bake in an oven preheated to 190°C/375°F/Gas 5 for 12 minutes. Take carefully off the baking paper and let them cool.

Yoghurt and Raisin Cupcakes ❄ ☺ ☹

The yoghurt and ground almonds keep these cupcakes lovely and moist. If you like you could spread the tops of the cakes with glacé icing, as in the Animal Cupcakes (page 198), although I prefer to leave them plain.

MAKES 12 CAKES

150 ml/5 fl oz pot natural yoghurt
3 eggs, lightly beaten
1 teaspoon vanilla extract
175 g/6 oz golden caster sugar
140 g/5 oz self-raising flour
100 g/4 oz ground almonds
1 teaspoon baking powder
a good pinch of salt
175 g/6 oz butter, melted
75 g/3 oz raisins

Preheat the oven to 190°C/375°F/Gas 5. Line a 12-hole muffin tin with paper cases.

Put the yoghurt, eggs and vanilla extract in a jug and mix together. In a large bowl, combine the sugar, flour, ground almonds, baking powder and salt and make a well in the centre. Pour in the yoghurt mixture and the melted butter and quickly fold in the dry ingredients. Take care not to overmix. Finally, toss the raisins in a little flour and fold into the mixture.

Spoon the batter into the paper cases. They will be quite full. Bake for 18–20 minutes or until risen and springy to the touch. Cool for a few minutes and then transfer to a wire rack to cool completely.

My Favourite Chocolate Biscuit Squares ☺ ☹

These are great for a children's party or teatime treat. You could use just milk chocolate or plain chocolate if you prefer, and you could use only digestive biscuits. You can also substitute some mini marshmallows for the dried apricots.

MAKES 16 CHOCOLATE BISCUIT SQUARES

100 g/4 oz digestive biscuits
100 g/4 oz ginger biscuits
150 g/5 oz milk chocolate
100 g/4 oz plain chocolate
85 g/3 oz golden syrup
85 g/3 oz unsalted butter
100 g/4 oz ready-to-eat dried apricots, chopped
50 g/2 oz raisins
40 g/1½ oz Rice Krispies

Lightly grease and line a 20 cm/8 inch square shallow tin. Break the biscuits, place in a plastic bag and crush with a rolling pin to form coarse crumbs.

Melt the chocolate, syrup and butter in a heatproof bowl over a saucepan of simmering water. Alternatively, melt in a microwave on High for 2½–3 minutes, stirring halfway through. Stir in the biscuit crumbs until well coated, then add the chopped apricots and raisins and, finally, stir in the Rice Krispies.

Spoon the mixture into the prepared tin. Level the surface, pressing down with a masher, and put in the fridge to set. Cut into squares before serving.

Index

Acknowledgements

I am indebted to the following people for their help and advice during the writing of this book.

Margaret Lawson, Senior Lecturer in Paediatric Nutrition, Institute of Child Health; Professor Charles Brook, Consultant Paediatric Endocrinologist, Middlesex Hospital; Dr Sam Tucker FRCP, Consultant Paediatrician, Hillingdon Hospital; Dr Tim Lobstein, specialist in children's food and nutrition at The London Food Commission; Carol Nock SRN FCN, Midwife.

Thanks also to: Jacqui Morley; Mary Jones; Elizabeth Jones; Caroline Stearns and Aurelia Stearns, my stunning cover girl, plus all the babies and their parents who helped with the photography for this edition. Everyone at Ebury, especially Sarah Lavelle, Vicky Orchard, Carey Smith and Fiona Macintyre; everyone at Smith & Gilmour for their lovely design; Dave King for his beautiful photography; Nadine Wickenden for the gorgeous illustrations. My mother, Evelyn Etkind, for all her encouragement in writing this book. David Karmel, for his patience in teaching me how to use a computer. And, most important of all, my husband Simon, my chief guinea pig, for all his support.

If you enjoyed this book why not move on to recipes from my books for older babies and children?

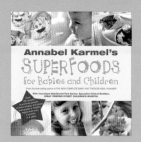

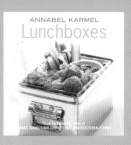

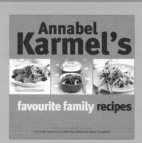

Superfoods for Babies and Children
Indispensable advice and recipes for children aged six months to five years.

Lunchboxes
Tips and great recipes for your child's lunchbox to ensure they always have a healthy, tasty meal at lunchtime.

Favourite Family Recipes
150 stress-free, mouth-watering recipes for both kids and their parents. Put the joy back into everyday cooking with this essential collection of tried and tested favourite recipes.

After-School Meal Planner
Make after-school meals and snacks easy with the essential planner that every parent needs. Packed with recipes and nutritional advice.

About the Author

Annabel Karmel is the leading author on cooking for children and has written 15 bestselling books that are sold all over the world, including *Top 100 Baby Purees* and *The Fussy Eaters' Recipe Book*. After the tragic loss of her first child, who died of a rare viral disease aged just 3 months, Annabel wrote her first book, *The Complete Baby and Toddler Meal Planner*, now an international bestseller with over one million copies sold. A mother of three, she is an expert in devising tasty and nutritious meals for children without the need for parents to spend hours in the kitchen. Annabel was the food consultant to Marks and Spencer when they launched their children's range in 2000 and more recently Annabel has successfully launched her own range of food and cooking equipment. Annabel was awarded an MBE for services to child nutrition in 2006. Annabel writes regularly for national newspapers and magazines and appears frequently on radio and television as the UK's top expert on children's nutritional issues. To buy other titles by Annabel Karmel, visit www.randomhouse.co.uk or Annabel's own website, www.annabelkarmel.com.

annabel karmel

Annabel Karmel's
make your own ...

I recognise that how you feed your baby is one of the most important decisions you make for your child, so I have devised a new range of equipment and food to help you. The range provides everything you need to make fresh food for your baby or toddler. It includes:

- **Baby Food Grinder**
- **Electric Hand Blender**
- **Food Cube Trays**
- **Rocket Ice Lolly Moulds**
- **Sauces and Pastas**

All are available from **Boots** stores and from **www.Boots.com**. For delicious recipes from the range, visit my website **www.annabelkarmel.com**

annabel karmel says
eat fussy

It's good to be a bit fussy about what you eat these days. That's why I have created a new range of tasty, yet healthy meals made especially for children. They're balanced, mouth-watering meals for young children aged 1 to 4 without the fuss. What's more, I'm very fussy about what goes into them so I only use the best natural ingredients.

- **Scrummy Chicken Dumplings with Rice**
- **Mummy's Favourite Salmon and Cod Fish Pie**
- **Beef Cottage Pie**
- **Yummy Chicken Curry**
- **Hidden Vegetable Pasta**
- **Cheeky Chicken and Potato Pie**
- **Teddy Bear Pizzas**
- **Meatballs with Spaghetti and Tomato Sauce**

Look for **Eat Fussy** in the chilled section of your local supermarket: just ask!